W9-CQF-011
253
h

SHARING JESUS

What Witnessing Is Really All About

By Jean Sheldon

PACIFIC PRESS PUBLISHING ASSOCIATION

Mountain View, California
Oshawa, Ontario

1—S.J.

4010

Copyright © 1981 by
Pacific Press Publishing Association
Litho in United States of America
All Rights Reserved

Cover and design by Ichiro Nakashima

Library of Congress Cataloging in Publication Data
Sheldon, Jean, 1956-
  Sharing Jesus.

  Includes bibliographical references.
  1. Witness bearing (Christianity)
2. Seventh-Day Adventists—Doctrinal and
controversial works. I. Title.
BV4520.S45   248'.5   79-27841
ISBN 0-8163-0350-9

Table of Contents

Preview

If you are young in body
   or in spirit;
If you are a born-again Christian,
   afire with the love of God;
If you have a burning desire
   to share the good news about Him
      with others—

Then
Come along with me,
And we'll sit down and talk
   and plan and dream together
On that huge old rock over there—
The one leaning up
   against the cross.

Napa
Seventh-Day Adventist
Church Library

By Definition

Directions: Circle all the right possibilities.
WITNESSING IS—

1. Singing "Happiness Is the Lord" while walking down a city street.
2. Putting a "7 SDA" personalized license plate on your car.
3. Smiling at all you meet (whether they know you're a Christian or not).
4. Placing a *Do You Have the Mark of the Beast?* pamphlet in a plane magazine pocket.
5. Asking advice from a non-Christian friend.
6. Giving rewards to those who bring people to evangelistic meetings.
7. Finding the right text to prove baptism by immersion.
8. Asking sincere questions about God of a Jesus person.
9. Helping your next-door neighbor get his car started on Sabbath.
10. Asking a stranger, "If you knew that you

were going to die tonight, would you have the assurance of salvation?"

11. Admitting that you have sinned.
12. Taking a good-natured poke at Sunday keepers.
13. Crying with a person who is hurting inside.
14. Letting someone choose to not be a Christian.
15. Singing at a nursing home on Tuesday afternoon.
16. Refusing to eat meat because "I'm a Seventh-day Adventist!"

Right Church, Wrong God

Our college communications instructor tossed us this question to begin our first class in Mass Media: "How many ways can a person communicate by sleeping?"

Communicate by *sleeping?*

How can anyone communicate by sleeping? That's when all communication stops!

The teacher broke into our surprise and confusion. "The point I'm trying to make is that there is no such thing as 'noncommunication.' You cannot *not* communicate. You've probably heard someone say something like this: 'I simply can't communicate with her.' That's nonsense! No matter what you do or say you are communicating something, whether you're aware of it or not. Even your sleeping habits communicate something about you.

"Now, there is negative communication and also positive communication. When a man refuses to speak to his wife, he may be communicating that he is mad at her. That is negative communication. When I smile at you, I am communicating that I like you. That is positive communication."

After class I pondered his words. If there is no such thing as noncommunication, I decided, perhaps there is also no such thing as a nonwitness.

True or False: Witnessing is something you do on Sabbath afternoons. False! Witnessing is something you do every day of the week—whether you want to or not. Everybody who professes to be a Christian is automatically a witness.

To every person you meet, you are saying something about the kind of God you worship. Of course, what you communicate about Him may be positive or negative. Depending on what you say and the kind of person you are, the picture of Him you give to others will be beautiful and correct, or it will be ugly and wrong.

If you cheerfully clean the room for your roommate even though it isn't your turn, you witness to a gracious God. If you tell your non-Adventist friend that he'd better keep the Sabbath or he'll probably be lost, you witness to a god who is arbitrary and vengeful.

Great—someone says. If witnessing is mainly living, then can't I just forget joining the singing band, telling a story at the story hour, or painting a poor family's house? Doesn't this mean there's no need to give Bible studies or bring a nonbelieving friend to an evangelistic service?

That's right! *If* you want to say Amen to the devil's lies about God!

One of the biggest tales Satan has ever told human beings is that God is heartlessly unconcerned about people. But if you never actively endeavor to tell the truth about God, others looking on could well conclude that you agree that God doesn't care.

If you really do know the truth about God—that He is not the kind of Person Satan has made Him out to be—you will be eager to correct the wrong pictures of God that torment so many people. You will be a very active witness. But your witnessing will be natural and spontaneous—not forced. Jesus didn't say, "Strain as hard as you can to make your light shine." He said, "*Let* your light . . . shine."[1]

"Who can by faith behold the wonderful plan of redemption, the glory of the only-begotten Son of God, and not speak of it? Who can contemplate the unfathomable love that was manifested upon the cross of Calvary in the death of Christ, that we might not perish, but have everlasting life—who can behold this and have no words with which to extol the Saviour's glory?"[2]

If you know and admire God, you won't be able to keep from telling and showing others what He's really like.

In witnessing the most important question is, "What kind of God are we witnessing about?" Is our God long-faced, or does He smile a lot? Are His commands unreasonable, or is He a delight to obey? Does He like to argue about the truth, or is He patient with someone who doesn't want to listen to His side of the question?

Too often our foremost goal seems to be to "get them into the church." It sometimes doesn't seem to matter what helps them decide—as long as they decide to be Seventh-day Adventists! If the approach works to get their names on the church books, it must be OK.

But how many of the people we baptize each year come into the right church worshiping the *wrong God?*

If we could be in heaven right now, perhaps we would see an angel pressing reverently in before God. With bowed head and tear-stained face, he says, "Father, years ago You promised that before Jesus went back to earth there would be a new group of people who perfectly represented You.[3] They would know You so well that You could say, 'Here they are! Here are those who are like Me. If you want to know what I am like, look at them. I can trust them to defend My reputation fearlessly no matter what; they will never let Me down.'

"Where are they, Father? I know that Your promise will be kept, but we've waited almost 140 years. How much longer?"

The world's millions are also asking questions. They want to know if God would tell a neighbor that her well-groomed lawn is beautiful. Would He pick up a tousled-haired youngster who has fallen (after throwing a clod at His house) and, while kindly asking him not to throw things, dry his tear-stained face? Would He comfort the woman up the street, the mother with six children who just lost their daddy?

12

Would He, in giving Bible studies, allow His students to ask any questions about Himself they wanted to? Even if the questions seemed rebellious? Even if it were the fourth time they had been asked?

What the world needs most is the kind of witnessing that tells and shows the truth about God.

In everything we say and do, as we witness, we must ask ourselves these questions:

What are we saying about our God?

Is it true?

Does it answer the questions people are asking about Him?

Notes and References

1. Matthew 5:16, emphasis supplied.
2. Ellen G. White, *Thoughts From the Mount of Blessing,* pp. 43, 44.
3. See Ellen G. White, *Christ's Object Lessons,* p. 69.

"The Truth,
the Whole Truth,
Nothing but the Truth"

Suppose you are in court as a witness to an accident you saw happen. You have just sworn to tell "the truth, the whole truth, and nothing but the truth." The prosecuting attorney asks you the first question: "Which car did you see turn left?"

Suddenly your mind goes blank. Which car *did* turn left? The green car or the VW? Maybe neither car turned left, and the lawyer is simply trying to trip you up.

How will you be able to tell the truth? You did see it happen, didn't you? Well, since you've apparently forgotten, perhaps you can just guess which car turned left. But would that be telling "nothing but the truth"?

Do we know the truth—the truth that makes us Seventh-day Adventists? Or have we forgotten what it really is? Worse yet, have we perhaps never known?

Certainly we know something *about* the truth. We know that the seventh day is the Sabbath, that Jesus is coming again soon, that the dead are asleep in their graves, that we were created by God, that the Bible is inspired. Is that enough?

Would it have been enough back when the great controversy began?

If the most trusted executive in God's government had begun to tell you subtle lies about God—that God was really dishonest, unfair, and arbitrary—would you have believed him? A good share of the angels did.

In fact, Ellen White points out that even the loyal angels were so influenced by Satan's lies that, before Christ came to this earth, they waited for God to get angry with Satan and his rebels and destroy them.[1]

Because of this and because God wants to win man back, He has spent the last six millenniums trying to explain and demonstrate the truth about Himself. At the cross the evidence that God is nothing less than gracious, fair, and honest was so overwhelming that the angels could clearly see that God was the Victor.[2]

Down here, however, the lies about God are still multiplying. People either worship a careless, unconcerned deity or else a god waiting to pounce on their every misdeed in order to burn them in hell. Even the Bible has been misused to persuade people that God is an unmerciful tyrant. How can God reveal more clearly the truth about Himself?

I believe that God has, in a *special way*, asked us to explain and demonstrate to the world the truth about God. In a *special way*, because He

15

has asked that the last generation of believers grow up into full maturity and demonstrate the truths about God which they profess to believe.

Paul tried to get the people of his day to do this, especially those facing the destruction of Jerusalem. "Let us leave behind the ABC of Christ and not lay again a foundation of repentance from dead works, faith in God, teaching about baptisms, laying on hands, raising the dead, and everlasting judgment," he wrote. "But let us go on to be mature."[3]

But tragically those early Christians didn't continue to know God more perfectly. Lies about God began to insert themselves into the truth. Soon the lies were accepted as the truth, and terrible things were done in the name of Christ.

Even though the Reformation resulted in a tremendous breakthrough, by 1844 confusion abounded among Christians even in the Protestant churches. Some still believed that God forced babies to become Christians whether they wanted to be or not. Others interpreted God's graciousness to mean that His law was arbitrary and useless. Many believed that God derived great satisfaction from burning wicked souls forever and ever.

How could God persuade Christians to believe and spread the truth about Himself?

That is why the year 1844 marks such a cataclysmic turning point in Christendom. Many of the Millerites after the Great Disappointment had no denominational home. Those who refused to give up their faith in Jesus and began to understand that He was to cleanse the heavenly sanctuary met in small groups to study the Bible. And it was in these small groups that they began to rediscover all of the truth about God that Jesus had revealed. Bringing with them the truths they had learned in their former churches, they began to put these scattered truths together into one body.

They established the fact that God's Sabbath is not a legalistic, arbitrary day of rest that ended at the cross. Instead, it is bound up in His character and reflects His creative and re-creative power.

They discovered that God would not eternally burn His wicked creatures in hell but would bring all sin and suffering to an end.

They agreed that the God of the Old Testament is the same as the God of the New; both are equally gracious.

All the truths they brought together and made clear are part of the eternal good news about God.

Why was it so important that these truths be focused upon in 1844 and shortly thereafter?

Because now Jesus could begin His final work of reconciling His people in this world without being misunderstood. Now He could plead for His people in an investigative judgment without their fearing that He would have to plead with the Father to accept and love them. Knowing God as they now did, they could approach His throne with confidence; they had learned that God would do all He could to save them.

Realizing that the dead were not already in either heaven or hell, God's people felt that the investigative judgment made sense. Convinced that the law was still intact, that it was not burdensome but reasonable, they could accept it as the standard describing the lives of those whom God could allow in heaven.

More than that, Jesus could now begin His final work of restoring His people so that they perfectly reflected His character. Then the world could see Him, as He really is, in His followers.

And how is this done?

Jesus, in His prayer to His Father, said, "Sanctify them through thy truth: thy word is truth."[4]

Paul added: "We all, with unveiled face, beholding the glory of the Lord, are being changed into his likeness from one degree of glory to another."[5]

And Ellen White observed: "It is a law both of the intellectual and the spiritual nature that by beholding we become changed. The mind gradually adapts itself to the subjects upon which it is allowed to dwell. It becomes assimilated to that which it is accustomed to love and reverence."[6]

It is through a correct understanding of the truth about God that we come to love, trust, and admire Him. And as we understand that truth more fully and admire God more completely, we are transformed to become like Him.

But it wasn't until 1844 that the full truth about God began to be clearly seen. Most people during the Dark Ages couldn't reflect His perfection, because of their false and imperfect picture of Him. Their god was a tyrant, and history reveals the painful fact that too many of them became tyrannical just like him. Even many in Reformation times didn't move on to understand fully the truth about God.[7]

That is why God brought together a whole new movement through which He could reveal all the good news. A new movement which could become like the God Jesus represented. *Every truth we have the privilege of sharing with others is a truth about God.* And God has asked us to give every person on earth an opportunity to hear that truth and see it demonstrated in human lives.

"It is the darkness of misapprehension of God that is enshrouding the world. Men are losing their knowledge of His character. It has been misunderstood and misinterpreted. At this time a message from God is to be proclaimed, a message illuminating in its influence and saving in its power. His character is to be made known. Into the darkness of the world is to be shed the light of His glory, the light of His goodness, mercy, and truth. . . .

"Those who wait for the Bridegroom's coming are to say to the people, 'Behold your God.' The last rays of merciful light, the last message of mercy to be given to the world, is a revelation of His character of love. The children of God are to manifest His glory. In their own life and character they are to reveal what the grace of God has done for them.

"The light of the Sun of Righteousness is to shine forth in good works—in words of truth and deeds of holiness."[8]

We are on the witness stand, not to give evidence concerning an accident, but to give evidence that God is not the kind of Person Satan has claimed He is. Depending on our picture of God, our witness will be correct, or it will back up Satan's lies.

Hopefully, we will so know and love God that, in what we say about Him and in the way we live, we will tell "the truth, the whole truth, and nothing but the truth" about our God.

Notes and References

1. Ellen G. White, *That I May Know Him,* p. 19; *The Desire of Ages,* p. 37.
2. Ellen G. White, *The Desire of Ages,* pp. 758-764.
3. Hebrews 6:1-3, W. F. Beck.
4. John 17:17.
5. 2 Corinthians 3:18, R.S.V.
6. Ellen G. White, *The Great Controversy,* p. 555.
7. See Ellen G. White, *The Story of Redemption,* pp. 353-355.
8. Ellen G. White, *Christ's Object Lessons,* pp. 415, 416.

Where the Power Comes From

We sat in a circle trying to answer the question we had formed this committee to solve: How can we get our academy to have a revival?

Just a few months before, a few of us students had experienced a revival. But already the flame of enthusiasm flickered fatefully low, and we felt the need of rekindling. So, inviting Mrs. Boyle, a staff member's wife, about half a dozen of us gathered, hoping to find the fuel.

Jerry came in as we searched the Bible for ideas that would help us. He sat next to Mrs. Boyle and listened. Since he wasn't known to be particularly religious, we figured he was there seeking something new to fill a boring Sabbath afternoon.

But Mrs. Boyle sensed in Jerry a longing to know God as His personal Friend. Quietly—unnoticed by the rest of us—she talked understandingly to him, reassuring him that God loved him just the way he was.

Suddenly conviction came, and Jerry sobbed out his repentance. He wanted God's forgiving love and restorative healing.

Meanwhile, oblivious to anything unusual, we continued looking in our Bibles to find out about the revival among the early Christians. No one seemed able to discover the "right" verses. We closed our Bibles, and our discussion flickered feebly.

Suddenly Mrs. Boyle's voice interrupted us. "Here you are, trying to find ways to convert your fellow students to Christ," she said, "and yet you fail to sense the Holy Spirit's working right here in this room."

Stunned, we stared at her.

"You nearly missed your first convert—one in your own group," she continued. And she told us about Jerry.

Not until after we had separated did the full impact strike home. Who initiates conversion? We or the Holy Spirit? The Holy Spirit, of course. We couldn't revive students on our campus. Only He could. And later He did, using various *other* people.

Jesus told His disciples to wait at Jerusalem for the outpouring of the Spirit.[1] "When the Holy Spirit comes upon you, you will be filled with power, and you will be witnesses for me."[2]

That didn't mean that they were simply to huddle in the upper room waiting for some dramatic transformation to take place. On the contrary, they spent a portion of every day praising God in the temple.[3]

But when were the 3000 converted? *After* the Spirit came upon them.[4] Of themselves the disciples couldn't win one soul. Apart from the Spirit all the good words in the dictionary couldn't help them. Without Him even their most loving ministry would ultimately be ineffective in winning people to God.

That doesn't mean, however, that the Holy Spirit doesn't need us. His primary means of converting sinners is truth and love. And who could be better instruments for revealing that truth and love than re-created sinners?

All too often we think of the Holy Spirit as a "Power Center" instead of a Person. If we could just get more of the Spirit's power, we say, our witnessing would be more effective. We frequently tend to think of our wonderful Comforter and Friend as a slot machine: just push in three quarters' worth of prayer and ten dimes' worth of Bible study, and out will come power for witnessing.

All this makes us the "control center" to use the Holy Spirit. He becomes, to us, a robot to meet our demands. When this happens, the Divine Counselor cannot do much to help us. He will certainly never force His way into our committee meetings and say, "Your witnessing programs must be conducted *My* way, or else!" *We* may do that, but He never will. Instead, He graciously seeks to speak through our minds to give us advice and instruction. He hopes that we will let Him help us correctly interpret the guidelines He has given in His Word.

But when we refuse to go His way, He sadly lets us stubbornly cling to our pet theories and programs. If the results are disastrous (as they usually are without His guidance), they make God look bad. Yet the Spirit still seeks to use us.

Many times we limit the Holy Spirit by restricting Him to only a few narrow avenues of reaching people with the good news. Sometimes we are not open to new methods or new instruments (people) that He would like to use. If a new idea doesn't fit into our trusty 3×5 card file, for example, can it be of much value? Or if it doesn't net any immediate baptisms, it must not be working.

But knowing the power and patience of our God, we can understand that His Spirit will use every avenue He can to convince people that God is love. Would that we were more open to and better understood the good news ourselves!

The Holy Spirit longs most for loving and lovable Christians. Christians who do not oppose Him by misrepresenting God but who seek every opportunity to defend God's reputation.

As our Counselor and Friend the Spirit longs to walk everywhere with us so that whenever we meet someone who doesn't know God, that person will sense His loving presence. In fact, just His unseen influence surrounding us may bring about the initial breakthrough.

Debbie had been attending church several weeks with my folks when I met her. Her first contact with Adventism had come through her next-door neighbors, who had invited her to attend church with them. Since we lived about a block down the street, we were asked to continue helping Debbie when her neighbors no longer could.

Debbie was about my age, and when I came home from college, she came over quite often to visit. When I decided to visit her, I wondered how her family would react. I knew her parents were opposed to her becoming an "Advent."

Sure enough, the atmosphere was definitely cool. Her dad sat in his overstuffed chair, puffing on a cigarette, watching TV, and only barely acknowledging my presence. Her mom hardly spoke to me, and her brothers acted as if I were part of the wall paneling. I stayed only ten minutes, then left.

A while later, when I found myself in her living room again, the temperature was two degrees warmer.

About the fifth time I visited Debbie, she was alone with her dad, who was recovering from open-heart surgery. He still sat in his favorite chair, smoking and watching one TV program after another—some of which were not the kind I'd voluntarily turn to. Not wanting to be impolite, I watched, deciding to stay a half hour.

Later, on my way home, I complained to the Lord, "What kind of soul winning was that? I didn't even get a chance to say a word about You!"

Suddenly I realized that just my being in that non-Christian home had given the Holy Spirit a chance to be there too. And that family had undoubtedly sensed His presence.

The next time that I entered Debbie's living

room her dad greeted me with a warm smile, and I knew the temperature had soared. Today Debbie is a Seventh-day Adventist, and her parents show indications that the Spirit is working on their hearts.

When the Holy Spirit is our Teacher, Guide, and Sustainer, our witness becomes far more adaptable to different people. The Holy Spirit works with individuals, not masses. When an evangelist presents the good news, the Spirit is beside each person in the audience seeking to convince and persuade him. When someone picks up a book about our loving God, the Spirit adapts the message to that individual's experience.

As we ourselves experience His influence, our endeavors to win others become so spontaneous and natural that fear, embarrassment, and tension disappear.

During my junior year of academy a friend and I spent several afternoons with a lay activities director visiting people who were receiving *Signs of the Times.*

One lady, a Mormon, greeted us warmly when she learned we were representatives of *Signs.* Soon our conversation centered around her boy and girl, junior age, who couldn't seem to get along with each other. Knowing how this must particularly distress a home-oriented Mormon, I told how Christ had come into our home and had smoothed out a similar difficulty. That seemed to give her courage.

We were about to leave when I said, "Could we

pray with you about your children?" At that moment it came out as effortlessly and naturally as saying, "Good morning!"

A smile lighted up her face and tears welled up in her eyes. "Please do!" she exclaimed, quickly opening the screen door. Soon we were kneeling in a circle in her living room.

From this experience I discovered that those who walk with the Spirit do not have to think, "Oh, dear, somehow I've got to pray with this person," or "I must make sure that everyone has a copy of this pamphlet."

Spirit-filled witnesses only need to make sure that they know God as He really is and that they've entrusted their lives to His guidance. Then they will be clear channels through which the Water of Life can flow.

Notes and References

1. Acts 1:4.
2. Acts 1:8, T.E.V.
3. Luke 24:53; Ellen G. White, *Acts of the Apostles,* p. 35.
4. Acts 2:1-41.

Paradox

What happens,
my friend,
when a dehydrated world
reaches out
for a drink of living water?

What happens
when we hand it
cups of overflowing water,
bubbling cool and clear?

What happens
when the world
stretches out parched lips
for that first desperate drink
that will revive it?

What happens,
my friend,
when just as it reaches
for that first sip,
it finds that the cups
are empty
from a leak?

Just a Cup of Water— That Doesn't Leak!

Carol, an academy junior, wasn't an Adventist when she attended a junior academy in California. She recalls her well-meaning friends who would say to her, "Hey, Carol, you shouldn't be doing this!" or "I certainly didn't think *you* would do that!" Carol remembers thinking, Yeah, but I know what you guys do every Saturday night!

Donna, an academy sophomore, became an Adventist about five or six years ago when she attended an Adventist elementary school in Maryland. She says that one of the major things that convinced her to become an Adventist was that Adventists "went by what they believed. If they were going to be vegetarians, they went all the way with it."

A friend of mine worked one summer with Campus Crusade Against Drugs. After days of heat-filled exhaustion, she wrote, "I ran into a lot of anti-Adventists. Most of them are down on us because we don't practice what we preach."

Is it true that we don't "practice what we

preach"? In what way? Is it important that we do what we say we should?

Suppose that every single Seventh-day Adventist stopped eating flesh foods, began going faithfully to church every Sabbath, stayed away from movies, and memorized five texts for each doctrine and teaching. Would they then be practicing what they preach?

The enigma of Christ's time was that those who fussed the most about the standards of their church were actually the biggest hypocrites! It was Simon, the Pharisee, you remember, who led Mary into adultery. And Jesus told the most religious people of His day that they were so busy worrying about microscopic matters that they "neglected the weightier matters of the law, justice and mercy and faith; these you ought to have done, without neglecting the others."[2]

Again, as is usually true, their basic problem was that they were worshiping the wrong god. Thus their witness was also of the wrong god.

Failure to follow our standards is also a symptom of worshiping the wrong god. When we compromise, we are actually blurring our picture of God. Those looking on conclude that His laws are unreasonable and too difficult to obey. If they could trust us to be consistent and genuine, our picture of God would mean a great deal more to them.

But it goes deeper than that. Many of our non-Adventist friends who watch us may figure that our message is about a system of beliefs and a rigamarole of standards rather than a gracious God. No wonder they are so quick to cry "Fraud!" when they see us not living up to our lists!

Of course, if we were known for the kind of God we worship, the risk of our failure to live up to that picture would be even greater. For perhaps our greatest problem lies in our failure to be loving and compassionate to one another and to those we try to win.

If people came to our church to look at our picture of God by watching us, what kind of picture would they see? Would they learn that our God is gracious to everyone? That He tries to make others happy and never says anything but the best about others? Or would they discover Him to be critical, unreasonable, impatient, unconcerned?

It is great to be the cups containing the water of life for a thirsty world. But if the cups leak, the world is bound to find out.

When we know and admire the right God and understand how sensible His laws are, we will find it delightful to do right. We will love others, for the essence of both God's character and His law is love.[3]

If this were true of us now, what would it do to our soul winning?

Throughout history one of the greatest reasons for the scorn shown Christians has been that they preach that God is love while hating others; that they frown instead of smiling; that they seem burdened with a list of arbitrary rules.

Conversely, Christians who love and smile and obey because they want to have exercised a tremendous power to attract others to Christ.

Carol found this true. It was the happiness reflected in Dave Meeker and Steve Marshall during a week of prayer that helped bring her to Christ. "I felt I didn't have what I wanted," she told me. "I was missing something." Then Steve and Dave came to the school and showed her the happiness that comes from knowing Jesus. And she wanted it.

Mr. Benner, now a denominational worker, found it easy to accept the Adventist message. But he was shocked when he discovered that not all of the fellows in the academy he attended had found the joy he had. They even made fun of him for taking spiritual things seriously, and his first year there was the most miserable one he'd ever had.

Donna had an opposite problem. Being a jewelry lover, she wore gold earrings to the Adventist elementary school she attended and was teased for wearing them. "You're a sinner!" her peers shouted. "You're going to burn in hell for doing that!" The last sentence they used the most!

I asked her if her friends were just giving her a bad time. "No," she said, "they were serious! They acted as if they were scared, too—like they were afraid that if they wore jewelry that they'd burn in hell." She added, "I was really afraid when they told me all this."

Fortunately, Donna had a really understanding teacher at that time who said, "Well, don't worry about it. Maybe when you accept the faith, you'll understand why we don't wear these things."

But her grandfather wasn't so fortunate. A heavy smoker, he went to church with Donna's parents—once. While in the narthex, he was given a big lecture on how he would go to hell for smoking. It turned him off. Completely. "He won't even think of becoming an Adventist now because of that," Donna said.

Love for sinners as well as for saints often makes an eternal difference. Had Donna's grandfather been given love instead of a sermon on health reform, he would not only have been more likely to quit smoking, but he would have found God a Person he could love.

Several teachers helping out in the kindergarten division of a Vacation Bible School found themselves struggling to cope with a little boy who seemed defiant about everything in the program. No one seemed able to get through to Jeffrey. By the middle of the second morning, the teachers realized they were nearing the end of their resources and needed God's concern for him. On their knees they pleaded that God would help them love Jeffrey, not merely discipline him.

It wasn't easy. But the change was almost immediate. Jeffrey began to respond to their love. By Friday morning he volunteered to pray before all of the other seventy children! At the graduation exercises Jeffrey received public recognition for helping one of the teachers with her nature projects. Afterward his aunt said, "That is the first time Jeffrey has ever heard a positive comment about himself!"

No wonder Paul put his beautiful comments about love in the middle of his discussion on spiritual gifts! Of all the Christian influences, love is the most important. If God is love, how can we correctly represent Him if we aren't loving ourselves?

A friend of mine, attending a day academy in central California, wrote me about the following incident:

"This fall a girl came to our school because she had heard that Christians were different than the kids in public school, and she thought these were the kind of kids she'd like to know.

"When she got here she was dressed in tight-fitting pants and a tight sweater that didn't quite meet in the middle. She had on many different kinds of make-up, and she talked like Archie Bunker.

"Well, all my good Christian friends clammed up in horror at this fine example of present-day heathenism. They teased her—and she laughed. And she left. The day she left she told the school counselor how she felt. How lonely and hurt she was. And she wasn't interested in 'Adventism' anymore!"

In Ellen White's words: "How little do we enter into sympathy with Christ on that which should be the strongest bond of union between us and Him—compassion for depraved, guilty, suffering souls! . . . The inhumanity of man toward man is our greatest sin. Many think that they are representing the justice of God while they wholly fail of representing His tenderness and His great love. Often the ones whom they meet with sternness and severity are under the stress of temptation. Satan is wrestling with these souls, and harsh, unsympathetic words discourage them and cause them to fall a prey to the tempter's power."[4]

Someday—and how our God must be longing for it!—He will have a group of people who give cups of clear, sparkling Water to a dehydrated world. Or better yet, they will *be* those cups, overflowing with the good news about their gracious God.

Best of all, those cups will not leak!

Notes and References

1. Because I wrote much of this chapter several years ago for an academy Bible class project, the dates and positions of the people I interviewed apply to that time and are not necessarily current.
2. Matthew 23:23, R.S.V.
3. 1 John 4:8; Galatians 5:13, 14.
4. Ellen G. White, *The Ministry of Healing,* p. 163.

Future Multiples

Directions: Choose as many as apply.

1. Which are the best kinds of crowns to wear?
   A. Crown of Rejoicing
   B. Crown of Stars
   C. Crown of Thorns

2. Which one will a born-again Christian wear first?
   A. Crown of Rejoicing
   B. Crown of Stars
   C. Crown of Thorns

3. Jesus will give each righteous person a Crown of Stars because:
   A. They've won souls, and each star represents a soul
   B. They deserve this award
   C. They've allowed God to work with them in helping His enemies become His friends
   D. Because He loves to do it for them; He loves to reward His people as though they have done it all

4. I will receive a star for each person God used me to win if:

A. That person never backs out of salvation
B. God used no one else to help win that person
C. I *know* exactly who that person is
5. The most important things in heaven are:
A. Being reunited with those I love
B. Finding out why certain trials had to happen to me
C. Seeing and talking to God (all three Persons)
D. Receiving a star-filled crown
E. Studying to learn more about God
F. Visiting other planets
G. Watching other people receive their crowns

Star Winning or Soul Winning?

Mary and I sat in our lay activities director's home waiting for him to take us to visit a Wayout contact. As academy students we had looked forward to this night and hoped that the contact would be responsive.

Before we left, our director sat on the sofa and talked to us. "You know," he said, "I knew a pastor once who admitted to me that he couldn't point to one person whom he could say he had won! Isn't it terrible that a minister of the gospel was so lukewarm he hadn't won anybody to the Lord?"

Eyes wide, Mary asked, "You mean you don't think he'll be saved?"

"I don't see how, Mary," he replied, shaking his head sadly.

As I walked out of his house that evening, I felt slightly chilly. I recalled how during my freshman year a classmate had asked a faculty member to tell her if she could possibly be saved. "I can't think of anyone who has been baptized as a result of my efforts," she confessed. "How can I make it to heaven if I don't have any stars in my crown?"

Since then I've heard the same concern expressed: A college friend who was relieved to discover that perhaps her "list of stars," in God's reckoning, was not as short as she had feared it was. A close relative who remembers vividly a pastor thundering from the pulpit, "How *many souls* have *you* won?"

While studying the subject of soul winning for my senior Bible class, I found this remarkable comment by Ellen White: "In this life, our work for God often seems to be almost fruitless. Our efforts to do good may be earnest and persevering, yet we may not be permitted to witness their results. To us the effort may seem to be lost. But the Saviour assures us that our work is noted in heaven, and that the recompense cannot fail."[1]

A friend my age recently decided to become a Seventh-day Adventist. Who will get her star? Her next-door neighbors who befriended her and were the first Adventists she knew? My folks who took her to church? The Bible worker who gave her studies? The editors and writers of the magazines she read? The pastor whose sermons she listened to each week? The Sabbath School superintendents? The evangelist in whose meetings she made her decision? The camp-meeting speakers she heard? The list could be endless!

But we have not mentioned yet three Persons without whom nothing would have happened: our heavenly Father, who poured out all heaven in love; Jesus, who came to reveal Him to us; and the Holy Spirit, whose ministry alone can make ours effective.

Who will get the credit? Will any wearing crowns deserve them? Or will they cast them at Jesus' feet?[2]

Why bother with stars and crowns at all? Are they really needed? God must feel that they are, perhaps for the same reason that the rewards given to the workers in the parable of the talents were needed.

"When the Master receives the talents, He approves and rewards the workers as though the merit were all their own. His countenance is full of joy and satisfaction. He is filled with delight that He can bestow blessings upon them. For every service and every sacrifice He requites them, not because it is a debt He owes, but because His heart is overflowing with love and tenderness."[3]

God rewards His people because He wants to and enjoys doing so. That is the kind of Person He is! He's just happy He has some people who can humbly handle His praise without expanding their egos. Those who receive the greatest awards will least expect them.

You remember the scene of the sheep and the goats that Jesus pictured for His disciples. To the sheep the King says, "Come, you who are blessed by my Father; take . . . the kingdom prepared for you since the creation of the world. For I was hungry and you gave me something to eat, I was thirsty and you gave me something to drink, ... I needed clothes and you clothed me, I was sick and you looked after me."[4]

And the "sheep" are surprised. "Lord," they say, "we don't remember doing any of those things!"[5]

This story used to bother me. Surely, some of the righteous "sheep" had read their Bibles and knew about this story, I used to think. How could they be surprised to hear what they had done? Why didn't they say instead, "Yes, Lord, of course that's right. Inasmuch as we did it unto the least of these, our brethren, we did it unto Thee!"[6]

Now I have the feeling that anyone who says that will be on the left hand! Genuine Christians will do loving deeds so naturally and spontaneously that they won't even think of a reward. Those who hear Christ speak those words will be thinking of Him, not of all the nice things they used to check off each week on the lay activities card!

But on the other hand, Jesus talked about some people who did many good things, yet will find themselves lost. Banging on heaven's door, they will cry, "Lord, let us in! Look at all the stars we've won! Why, Mary and Joe and Christine and Terry are inside the New Jerusalem. We gave them Bible studies! Why are we out here?"[7]

Why?

"I never knew you."[8]

How can that be? Of course He knew them. But what He will mean is, "You never really knew Me. You misrepresented Me by spreading the truth for the wrong reason."

When stars become more important than souls, it usually indicates that, again, we have misunderstood our God. And that misunderstanding results in less love for those we're trying to win.

Some of those I interviewed, who came from other denominational backgrounds, expressed doubt when I asked them, "Did you feel that the Adventists who worked with you were genuinely interested in you as a person? Or were they just interested in winning you to the church?"

Donna put it very bluntly. "I think they were just interested in chalking up one more person they'd won to the church because they didn't really seem to care that much at first. We'd ask them the question, 'Why?' and they'd say, 'Well, just because we say so.' "

In reaching for souls, is it possible that some of us sometimes get too concerned about reaching out and forget why or for whom we're reaching? Does the satisfaction we derive come from soul winning? Or does it come from star winning?

Our greatest satisfaction will come when we understand the truth about God and love as He loves. Then it won't matter so much whether or not we receive a reward. Future stars in our crowns will cease to worry us or make us proud.

My grandmother was a fairly shy little lady whom you'd never find giving Bible studies. But to those who knew her she was a never-failing friend, a source of comfort, someone they could trust to never gossip about their affairs. More than one of my friends adopted her as their grandmother. She seemed to know how to heal broken hearts, comfort withering souls.

Then, for the last four years of her life, Grandma lay immobilized in a nursing-home bed from a massive stroke. She could hardly see and couldn't speak or move. Many times we asked, "Why? What good can she be to the Lord and others in that condition?"

Ah, but we forgot something. Grandma could smile! And she did smile at everyone who came to see her. Who knows how many were helped by her smile? I can say, for one, that her smile during those awful days will never leave my memory to strengthen me in a paralyzing illness.

Sometimes I imagine the coronation soon to take place in heaven. I picture Grandma when Jesus places a crown full of glittering stars on her head.

"Jesus!" the shy little lady gasps. "That's not *my* crown! It couldn't be. Why, I can remember only one or two people I've helped to win. Surely You have the wrong person in mind! I never did anything much!"

And Jesus simply smiles and says, " 'As you did it to one of the least of these my brethren'— that little girl you were kind to, your warmth and kindness to the least or the greatest—'you did it to me.' "[9]

Notes and References

1. Ellen G. White, *Review and Herald,* July 11, 1912.
2. See Ellen G. White, *Early Writings,* p. 289.
3. Ellen G. White, *Christ's Object Lessons,* p. 361.
4. Matthew 25:34-36, N.I.V.
5. See Matthew 25:37-39.
6. See Matthew 25:40.
7. See Matthew 7:22.
8. Matthew 7:23.
9. Matthew 25:40, R.S.V.

How to Drive a Dismantled Car

You've been lazying around your room, trying to avoid studying, when the phone rings. Terrific! You reach for the receiver. It's Joe, one of your friends.

"Hey, you know what I've got?" he asks. Before you can answer, he adds, "A brand-new Trans Am!"

"Wow!" you reply, trying not to be envious. "Could I, uh, come over and see it?"

"Well, you know, that's really why I called you!"

Bang! The receiver drops into the hook, and you are on your way!

When you reach Joe's front yard, you notice something is strange. There's the car all right, but it's in parts strewn all around the lawn. Near the rosebushes are the steering wheel, a hub cap, the gasoline tank, and the backseat. Around the blue spruce lie the heater, three tires, the transmission, and the dash. As near as you can tell, the crankcase, the front seat, the shocks, and the rearview mirror are neatly lined up by the hedge. Many of the parts are apparently missing, including the engine, which you don't see anywhere.

"Isn't she a beauty?" mushes Joe.

"Are you crazy, man?" you blurt incredulously, "How do you expect to drive it? Where's the steering column? Where's the engine?"

Joe reaches for a tire. "Well, I've got this wheel here, and there's the transmission over there, and—"

"But you can't drive a car with just a wheel and a transmission!" you splutter.

Perhaps my hypothetical illustration seems ludicrous, but unfortunately such dismantling happens all too frequently in the church, the body of Christ.

In too many cases we've strewn around and even discarded many of the talents we have in our midst. Our tendency has been to separate all the forms of evangelism from one another. One well-defined area we have marked "public evangelism," which is often limited to speaker-to-audience relationships. Another is slotted "one-to-one witnessing," which usually consists of meeting people on Sabbath afternoons. Still another is labeled "medical evangelism," which throws pictures of hospitals, rehab centers, Five-Day Plans to Stop Smoking, and weight-control classes on our mental screens. Well off to the side are vague pictures of interpersonal relationships: sponsoring a student at an Indian mission, comforting a sorrowing child, smiling at the neighbors, etc. But these seem too far down the list, and they bother us because they aren't as easy to define and tabulate.

Concerning this very topic, Paul wrote, "The body [as is the church] is a unit, though it is made up of many parts; and though all its parts are many, they form one body. So it is with Christ."[1]

Ezekiel saw the same type of unity in the body of Christ in heaven. It was pictured as wheels working together in complexity, yet unity; separation, yet togetherness.[2]

Togetherness. How does it happen? How can the body of Christ make every member feel important and needed?

Unfortunately, some believe that there are only certain ways to witness. Perhaps you've gone to a church where only one method of witnessing was promoted. And the message you get is that "It's your duty to witness for the Lord. Therefore, you ought to participate in *this* program!"

Yet there is nothing more discouraging to many people than to feel guilty and condemned because they simply don't have talents for certain heavily promoted projects. They are likely to feel rejected by both the church and God.

Paul says, "There are varieties of gifts. . . . There are varieties of service. . . . There are many forms of work, but all of them, in all men, are the work of the same God. In each of us the Spirit is manifested in one particular way, for some useful purpose."[3]

"In all the Lord's arrangements," wrote Ellen White, "there is nothing more beautiful than His plan of giving to men and women a diversity of gifts. The church is His garden, adorned with a variety of trees, plants, and flowers. He does not expect the hyssop to assume the proportions of the cedar, nor the olive to reach the height of the stately palm."[4]

If you don't have a talent for teaching small children, don't feel that God is asking you to teach a kindergarten Vacation Bible School class. Find some area, like crafts, where you can help.

God is a God of diversity and freedom as well as a God of unity and self-control. He wants us to feel free to use only what He has given us, not what someone else feels we should use. As we use the gifts we do have, we will probably discover others we weren't aware of.

God needs all of us, no matter how insignificant our talents seem. "None need lament that they have not received larger gifts; for He who has apportioned to every man is equally honored by the improvement of each trust, whether it be great or small."[5] Ellen White intimates that even "the gift of sincere, earnest, fervent prayer" is one that some may have in greater degree than others.[6]

Isn't it true, though, that there are some fields of work more important than others, just as certain organs of the body have a greater work to do than others?

In a sense this is true. Even God recognizes

that personal witnessing "will accomplish more for the cause of Christ than can be wrought by sermons or creeds."[7] However, He doesn't look down on the evangelist as less important to His cause than the auto repairman who wins his customers. If the evangelist is best at preaching, then that's what God wants him to do.

Using Paul's example of bodily functions, the body can live without both legs, arms, and eyes. It can do without most of its stomach, the gall bladder, one of its kidneys, and one of its lungs. Yet even without only one of these members, the body is imperfect and cannot function as well as before.

"Now you are Christ's body, and each of you a limb or organ of it."[8] "Those organs of the body which seem to be more frail than others are indispensable, and those parts of the body which we regard as less honourable are treated with special honour."[9]

One part of the body that many of us who are young people need to treat with greater honor is the older generation. Unfortunately, the gap between talents and appropriate areas of service is often widened by the gap of the generations. Perhaps, since we are still considered young, we need to reevaluate our relationships with those older than we.

Paul wrote to Timothy, "Let no man despise thy youth."[10] Perhaps if he were writing now he would add, to the middle-aged and older, "Let no one despise thine age!"

Perhaps there are some seemingly soul-dampening adults who don't care to help in the witnessing adventures of young people. But then there are too many in the younger age-group who don't care to help either!

In most cases adults enjoy being asked for counsel and help. During my academy years a friend and I tried to start a rather large, visionary witnessing venture. One of the first things we did was to visit all the faculty and tell them about it. Many were a bit nonplussed, but nearly all of them nodded their heads, smiled, and said, "We'll pray for you," or "We hope you succeed." That meant a lot. Though the venture fell through, I still felt supported.

In the few years since, a number of other adults have helped me with witnessing and leadership projects. From them I gathered a wealth of learning—how to take hold, how to take the initiative, how to think things through.

The point is that everyone must feel needed and important in the body of Christ. Every person and talent should be used in the very best possible way.

Perhaps our biggest problem, though, is that we often forget the most important part of the body, the Head. When God's people focus on Christ, purposing only to present His picture of the Father, much of the machinery of evangelism—programs, methods, and people—will operate in harmony without wheels screaming and motors spluttering.

And as we study Jesus' picture of God humbly kneeling before twelve quarreling evangelists and washing their feet, perhaps we won't feel that our work is of greater or lesser importance than another's. Perhaps we will better understand the greatness of the lowest levels of service.

One of my favorite stories is of a washerwoman in London who while washing clothes, prayed every day for her son, John, who had run away to sea. There was nothing else she could do because she had no idea where he was.

But later, her son, John Newton, found Christ and became known as the Sailor Preacher of London. He won thousands of people to Christ. One of them was Thomas Scott, who won thousands more.

One of Scott's converts, Cowper, wrote the famous hymn, "A Fountain Filled With Blood," which touched many others, among whom was Wilberforce. Wilberforce not only won many souls, but helped inspire the empire to free its slaves. One man converted through his efforts wrote a book that was translated into more than forty languages and changed who knows how many lives.

When Jesus comes again, whose work will be seen as most important?

"The center of the whole thing," concludes the author, "an old woman—gray haired, bent back, stubby fingers—bending over the washing and ironing as she prayed for her boy, John. And praying until John came. . . . I am very clear about this, the Man on the throne yonder, who came from the throne to the cross and back, He

4010

would say: 'This woman, she was my friend. Through her prayer I could loosen out the power that touched untold thousands.' "[11]

Christ needs each of us now, using the talents we've been given.

"Diverse in mind, in ideas, one subject is to bind heart to heart—the conversion of souls to the truth, which draws all to the cross."[12]

Notes and References

1. 1 Corinthians 12:12, N.I.V.
2. Ezekiel 1:15-20.
3. 1 Corinthians 12:4-7, N.E.B.
4. Ellen G. White, *Evangelism*, pp. 98, 99.
5. Ellen G. White, *Christ's Object Lessons*, p. 328.
6. Ellen G. White, *Evangelism*, p. 99.
7. Ellen G. White, *Christian Service*, p. 12.
8. 1 Corinthians 12:27, N.E.B.
9. 1 Corinthians 12:22, 23, N.E.B.
10. 1 Timothy 4:12.
11. S. D. Gordon, "The Washerwoman's Prayer," *Prelude to Prayer* (Cincinnati, O.: The Standard Publishing Company, 1939). No page numbers are given in the booklet. Used by permission.
12. Ellen G. White, *Evangelism*, p. 99.

Inner City

Wall-to-wall concrete
carpets lonely prisoners' hearts
while sky-to-sky structures
blind their filmed eyes.
But even there,
above the raucous music
blaring from the fear of silence,
a voice speaks,
"Come to Me and rest."
And in between the forty-four stories
of disillusionment and distrust
He still stands,
blocking traffic back
across the tear-stained asphalt.
And there
with outstretched arms
He pulls apart
their neck-to-neck existence
and inserts love.

Out of the Adventist Ghetto

In an orthodontist's waiting room one afternoon, a little girl, about five, began looking through a copy of *The Bible Story* with her grandmother. Soon they came to a picture of Adam and Eve throwing down the forbidden fruit in the Garden of Eden.

"Why are they doing that?" asked the little girl.

"Because they shouldn't have taken it," her grandmother replied.

"Why?"

"Because God told them not to."

"God?" the girl puzzled. "What God? Which God?"

Silence.

"Is that God?" She pointed to Adam.

Longer silence.

"What God?" Urgency crept into the child's voice.

Her question hung in the air like a motionless cloud for a brief and uneasy moment. Then the grandmother, with hesitance born of ignorance, answered, "Our God in heaven, honey."

"O-h-h." The girl was doubtfully satisfied.

Children are not the only ones today asking, "What God?" In spite of the latest indications that America is still a "Christian nation," there are many to whom God is merely a swear word—to whom God is only for little old ladies and their grandchildren; and to many more, Christianity means little more than celebrating Christmas and Easter.

What are we going to do to reach these people? Wait for some other denomination to convert them to Christianity? Figure they are hopeless? Or launch out of our cozy Adventist ghettos to give them the good news?

Perhaps, in terms of definition, I'm stretching the word *ghetto* by using it to refer to Adventist "communities of contentment." Yet there are too many such areas whose boundaries are marked by little walls—social, religious, and intellectual—that make us feel "protected" from the world. Within these boundaries (especially on college and academy campuses) it is easy to talk among ourselves, enjoy a fairly unpolluted spiritual atmosphere, and never walk "outside."

Having been raised in the solidified atmosphere of Adventist ghettos (two different academy campuses where my father taught) for sixteen years, it used to be difficult for me to talk to a member of another Christian church. When it came to nonbelievers, the mental blocks were even higher.

During my senior year of academy my parents

moved to a suburb, and suddenly I found myself thrust into the middle of a seemingly hostile world. No longer was life cozy and secure. No longer could I talk freely to my neighbors about "the latest issue of *Insight*," "the Sabbath," "singing bands," etc.

Instead I had to smell dirty tobacco smoke and watch people drink beer. I had to contend with all the images I had built up in my mind about nonbelievers. How can I talk to them? I often pondered. They seem out of my range of conversation.

A year later, while attending Pacific Union College, I became involved in a witnessing venture called Berkeley Campus Ministries (B.C.M.). Early on Sabbath mornings we students would board a bus and head for the Berkeley Seventh-day Adventist church, located a few blocks from the well-known University of California campus. In the afternoons we would fan out all over the campus and invite anyone who was interested to come to a free meal being served in a health center not far away. While the guests ate, we would try to direct the conversation toward the object of the venture—Christ.

I will never forget my first Sabbath at Berkeley. Merged into the kaleidoscope of the "culture shock" I experienced were scenes of eastern-type outdoor markets on city sidewalks, a street preacher yelling through a minimike at passersby, a fellow standing on a street corner asking everyone, "Can you spare a dime?" Hare Krishnas, people milling around or wandering aimlessly, signs putting down the government, bulletin boards full of everything from ESP ads to yoga class announcements.

As I observed all the people—from pseudo-intellectuals to cult followers, from drug addicts to weary mothers—one thought became clear: in order to reach people, especially non-Christians, we must go where they are and understand as much as possible (without numbing our own spiritual senses) what they feel, opening our minds to their needs.

This is what Christ did, not because He had to find out what our needs were, but because it was the only way we could know Him as He really is.

"The prince of teachers, He sought access to the people by the pathway of their most familiar associations. . . . He taught in a way that made them feel the completeness of His identification with their interests and happiness. His instruction was so direct, His illustrations were so appropriate, His words so sympathetic and cheerful, that His hearers were charmed."[1]

Perhaps we need to follow His example better. It's easier to follow our own illusive trails. It makes us feel more secure to try to reach imaginary people with our preconceived problems attached to them, than to try to understand and know them as they really are.

One Sunday morning, as I listened to a religious radio station, I heard someone sing the song, "Something Good Is Going to Happen to You." As the last line faded—"Jesus of Nazareth is passing your way"—the speaker gushed, "If you knew from the bottom of your heart that Jesus Christ really was passing your way, you would be *so thrilled!*"

Suddenly I found myself, in the framework of a nonbeliever, thinking, "Oh, yeah, man? Just how do you know?"

To assume too much with people is to invite disaster. One of our biggest assumptions as Christians is that nonbelievers *want* to be Christians. "If you knew Christ, you would get so excited!" Eyebrows go up, and the person confronted with such a message wonders, "What reason do they have for saying that? All I remember about Christ is that He was a namby-pamby sissy who allowed people to walk all over Him and finally kill Him. I'm not excited about Him at all!"

We need to make sure that we always give people evidence that God is trustworthy. "God never asks us to believe, without giving sufficient evidence upon which to base our faith. His existence, His character, the truthfulness of His word, are all established by testimony that appeals to our reason; and this testimony is abundant."[2]

Our faith in God must never hint of superstition nor border on the senseless. Our faith in God must be rational, for He is rational. If such is the case, our witnessing will also be rational. No one will feel, after hearing about our God, that to believe in Him equals a fantastic jump into a great bottomless unknown.

In one of our informal rap sessions at the

health center in Berkeley, one of the fellows from off the streets declared arrogantly, "Jesus was a bum! He had hang-ups!"

"No," I protested, "Jesus wasn't a bum."

I wish I could do it again. Knowing what I've since learned, I would now say, "You're right! In the eyes of some, Jesus was a bum. But He was also God and came to show us what God is like. In order to do that, He went even farther than you suggest. He accepted the guilt of a criminal to show us how much He loved us."

As it was, one of my schoolmates near me caught my attention. "No, Jean," he whispered, "tell him he's right. Jesus did have a hang-up. His hang-up was love."

Quickly I switched tactics. "You're right," I said, "Jesus did have a hang-up. His hang-up was love, because He loved everybody."

That afternoon I learned the power of the good news. Had I attacked the fellow for not believing in God or had I expected him to believe that God was worthy of his faith without giving him evidence, he could have rightly become angry with me.

But as I said, "He loves everybody," the eyes that had sneered at me before now dropped and he shuddered visibly. Soon he got up and walked out to have a smoke.

To argue about Christ's status was safe enough, but to hear about His love was to confront reality. Anyone can walk away—maybe run—from a god who glowers down from heaven with a flaming sword. But one can't as easily walk away from a God who holds out two nail-pierced hands of love.

One of the greatest reasons I found in Berkeley for unbelief in God was not the question "Does God exist?" but "If God is, what is He like?" Many do not believe in God because they think of Him as distant or tyrannical.

Do we as Seventh-day Adventists have the answers to the world's misconceptions and questions about God? Yes. Have we been attempting to give them to people? Or have we been unaware that we have the answers? Have we been sure of those answers ourselves?

Perhaps the biggest symptom of the uncertainty about those answers pops out when we hide the good news behind difficult theological terms, pretentious jargon, and worn-out clichés. Granted, many of these phrases are found in both the Bible and Ellen White's writings. Yet to many of us they have become meaningless and repetitious. Worse yet, we often use them as weapons for word battles.

Words alone do not have the power to convert people to Christ. There must be meaningful and radiant truth behind our words. We must understand the truth so clearly ourselves that we can present it eloquently in the simplest way possible. Perhaps we're not aware that a new generation (some of whom attend church) is growing up, many of whom are completely lost with terms like "worship," "salvation," "righteousness," let alone words like "atonement," "sanctification," and "repentance."

Little three-year-old Troy evidently first heard about Jesus at a story hour. He sat through the stories about Him wide-eyed. When the teacher told the children, "Let's pray to Jesus," Troy said, "Hi, Jesus!"

Near the end of one afternoon's session, after puzzling over all the new ideas he'd heard about Jesus and prayer, Troy announced sweetly, "I'm going to get Jesus' telephone number!"

Troy is one of many who will soon be adolescents wondering about God. How are we going to reach them with the good news? Too many of the younger set do not picture God as a personal Friend, but as a far-off Power Center with wires stretching to the earth.

How, for example, do you reach the thirteen-year-old who, trying to be funny, calls up and finally admits, "I've just mowed all this weed, and I feel like I'm going off my rocker?" Do you tell him about Jesus? Do you pray for him?

I did that one night. Two days later he called back and asked, laughing, "Is this the Lord?"

Perhaps before we march out to give the good news to those like him, we need to pause to pray for understanding. Perhaps before we talk to the man on the street, we need to listen to him. Can we turn our ears on and our mouths off for a few moments to hear the subtle sounds of voices— voices crying for help, for love, for human dignity—ultimately crying for a correct picture of God? If we don't listen carefully, we will miss their undertones of despair; we will hear only the surface noise of disrespect and rebellion.

I tried listening one day at Berkeley. Listening and mingling. May I share with you what I heard and saw?

As I came onto the campus, I heard a lot of shouting. Curious, I walked over to a crowd of hecklers surrounding a short, stocky man with scraggly, thinning hair and several missing teeth. His name was Holy Hubert, and he had been at U.C. Berkeley for several years. A prominent street preacher, he spent his time witnessing to the street people of Berkeley and to U.C.'s students.

Right now he was standing on the steps leading to the campus center and shouting down condemnations upon the youth around him. "You don't love God!" he thundered, shaking his forefinger at them. "That's why you take drugs and have sex."

A tall, thin fellow with long blond hair drew closer to "Huby" (another of Holy Hubert's nicknames). "I'm happy the way I am!" he announced. "I want to see a better Christian; you're a second-rate one!"

He swaggered before the crowd. "They [Christians] said I'd drop dead, but I'm still here. What happened?" The crowd seemed to approve.

A black man, dressed in white, and wearing a skull cap, moved out in front of the crowd. "God is in all of you," he intoned slowly. "You hate people because you're ignorant of God in you. God is in you. That's why you have energy." His glassy eyes stared at the crowd, yet seemed to see no one.

The tall fellow strutted. "I have energy because I eat doughnuts!"

Finished with his brief sermon, the glassy-eyed voodoo walked slowly away. (I heard later that he came to the health center, where P.U.C. students prayed that God would free his demon-possessed body.)

Soon Holy Hubert resumed his message and tried to convince the crowd that the Bible is inspired. "How do you know, Huby?" the crowd shouted. "Did you go to college?"

"Yes!" he answered emphatically. "I got my doctorate at a university in Tennessee."

"What was your dissertation on, Huby?" a voice asked.

"His dissertation was on 'Misery in the Christian Way,' " another answered. " 'How to Promote Suffering in Christians.' "

Realizing that he was losing ground, Holy Hubert blazed to the crowd, "You hate Him!"

"I don't hate Him," protested the tall fellow. "How can I hate someone I don't believe in? I don't believe in anything up there."

"Where is He?" mocked another voice. "Point Him out in this crowd."

"Waste yourself away and play your game!" Hubert retorted.

"I love it! I love it!" shouted the tall one.

"If I don't believe in Christ, He'll kill me!" he sneered. And the crowd laughed.

Walking down the steps, Huby began to move away from the crowd that was gradually dispersing.

"I've tried voodooism, drugs, everything!" screamed the tall one. "The only thing you guys promise me is heaven!" The look on his face added the words he had not voiced: And what is heaven?

As Holy Hubert walked slowly away, he jabbed his forefinger toward him and denounced him with these words: "You're going to burn in hell!"

The tall one's response rang out in a desperate cry for help—in a voice filled with mingled false bravado, anguish, and despair. "Let me!" he flung the words at Holy Hubert. *"Let me go to hell in peace!"*

I left Berkeley that day, a new page in my notebook full of words, my head spinning with thoughts, my life full of heartbreak. Always before I had left part of myself in Berkeley, buried in the mire of human need. But that day I carried the need back to P.U.C., where it went everywhere with me like a heavy burden on my back.

What hurt most was not Holy Hubert's misrepresentation of God, the skeptical voices, the irreverence, or the misconceptions about Him. What probed the deepest with fingers of burning anguish was that we who have been given the privilege of distinctly sharing the good news about God were not out there (and everywhere) actively giving that good news.

Locked in my memory of that afternoon is the figure of a girl who pushed her way through the crowd to talk to Holy Hubert. Tugging several times at his sleeve, she finally got his attention.

"Huby," she urged. "Huby, what we really want to know is, 'Does God love us?'"

Huby never answered her question.

Have we?

Notes and References

1. Ellen G. White, *The Ministry of Healing,* pp. 23, 24.
2. Ellen G. White, *Steps to Christ,* p. 105.

Friend Winners

People are houses
with windows and doors.
Some Christians
try to win them
by climbing in through the windows.
They are considered thieves.

Other Christians
try to win them
by breaking down the house.
They are considered murderers.

Still others try
by banging in the front door.
They are considered intruders.

Finally,
there are those Christians
who simply knock gently
at the door.
When the door opens,
they let the people know
they care about them.
These are considered friends.

Start Here

We were going to war! Crouching in our narrow trenches, we waited eagerly to fire. There were about twenty of "us"—all from the same military academy, and only one of "them." We fingered our rifles and waited. This was what we were being trained for.

He fired first; but his bullet was soft, not meant to harm us. After all, he wasn't out to fight us. He was only trying to give us what he considered to be the truth.

But he didn't know that *we* had the truth. So we waited. Then someone fired from our side, and the war was on.

Bullet No. 1: "What do you think about Exodus 20:8-10?"

The "Jesus people" minister acted a little unsure of himself. "Well, what does Exodus 20:8-10 say?" he asked. "You repeat it to me."

Aha! He doesn't even know what it says!

Bullet No. 2: "It says, 'Remember the sabbath day, to keep it holy. Six days shalt thou labour, and do all thy work: but the seventh day is the sabbath of the Lord thy God.' "

The minister seemed a bit worried. "Well, ah, we believe that every day is the Sabbath."

Bullet No. 3: "But the fourth commandment says that only *one* day is the Sabbath—the seventh day—and that we shouldn't work on that day."

"Well, we are not under law but under grace."

Ah! We've got him now!

Bullet No. 4: "You mean we can be saved without keeping the law?"

The war continued, but I'm not sure that either side won.

I wonder what the minister must have thought about the God of Seventh-day Adventists when that session was through. Our meeting with him was not intended to be argumentative. He was there by the request of the Community Organization for Drug Abuse Control (C.O.D.A.C.) to help them with a workshop. Since the delegates to the workshop (high school students) were to be working with elementary school children, C.O.D.A.C.'s leaders decided that they should learn how to communicate effectively with different types of people.

Well, we communicated—but not about a gracious God.

I wonder if the minister (and other religious leaders we talked to that afternoon) noticed the we're-going-to-get-you gleams in our eyes. Did our "frontal attacks" make them more willing to listen to the good news? I doubt it.

What is revealed when we speak the truth?

That we're out fighting a "holy war"? Or that we're followers of the One who said, "I came that they may have life, and have it abundantly"?[1]

Certainly there is a time and place for discussion of the Sabbath and other equally heavy doctrines. But unless the subject is a common one to both parties, one needs to proceed cautiously.

This was our mistake with the "Jesus people" minister. If we had agreed with him when we could, rejoiced with him over the goodness of God, and shared with him our mutual faith in Jesus, we would have done much toward breaking down his prejudice. If we disagreed, we should have done so very tactfully, with a refreshingly God-centered approach. As it was, we only hurt him and his picture of our God.

Some time after this experience I found this surprising statement: "You should not feel it your duty to introduce arguments upon the Sabbath question as you meet the people. If persons mention the subject, tell them that is not your burden now. But when they surrender heart and mind and will to God, they are then prepared candidly to weigh evidence in regard to these solemn, testing truths."[2]

Too many times we take the counsel of Peter—"Be ready always to give an answer"[3]—to mean that whenever we get a chance we should speak up for the Sabbath. However, a closer look at his advice reveals that this isn't necessarily what he meant.

On the other hand, we are warned against

being too cautious and never presenting any controversial doctrine.[4] It is important, then, to keep open to teachable moments when the Spirit prompts us to move ahead.

Perhaps our most important question in this chapter is, Where do we begin? And how?

Jesus began with a Samaritan lady by asking her for a drink of water.

To Zacchaeus He invited Himself home to dinner.

A crippled man He asked, "Do you want to get well?"[5] and healed him.

And before the multitudes He quietly sat down and taught them about His Father.

These different starting points have five common denominators:

1. Jesus reached out with loving concern for people—individually and in groups.

2. He treated all with dignity and gave them self-worth.

3. He began at the point where they sensed a need.

4. He tried to break down their prejudices.

5. As soon as possible He led them to see His Father in a new and favorable light.

All of these points are necessary to winning souls to Christ. Let's disuss them more fully.

1. Jesus reached out with loving concern for individuals. Since we've already enlarged on this point earlier, we won't say much more. Whatever approach we use, our love for individuals must be genuine. And individuals must come first. If God chooses to spend as much time and energy to win one of our relatives as He might spend on an evangelistic series for 300, what is that to us? He values persons infinitely more than we do.

It follows, then, that the method used must fit the person. There is no such thing as a sure-fire method that will convert everybody. Methods have their place, but there must always be room for initiative and personal adaptation.

2. He treated everyone with dignity and gave them self-worth. Simon the Pharisee was won to Jesus because Jesus didn't embarrass him. Simon, you remember, invited Jesus and His disciples to dinner. During the meal, Mary, a former prostitute, crept in and lovingly anointed Jesus' feet with oil in an act of worship.

Even though he had been one of those partly responsible for her sin, Simon was aghast. "If He knew what kind of a woman she's been," he scowled, "He wouldn't let her touch Him!"

Jesus could have said, "Simon, shame on you for judging her like that! You were one of those who led her into prostitution!"

Instead He simply told a story which revealed to Simon—but not to the others—that Jesus read his heart. It was Jesus' protection of his human dignity that led Simon to become a loyal follower.[6]

Ellen White calls this "divine politeness"—one of God's characteristics.[7] And Jude says that God is polite even to His archenemy, the devil.[8]

Love is never rude, but is always courteous. Love never puts anyone down, but seeks to lift everyone up—not with enlarged egos, but with a sense of the way God treats them.

3. He began at the point where they sensed a need. It's easy to figure that, because a person *needs* something, he therefore *wants* that something. Unfortunately, this is often not true. A man may need to stop smoking, but he may not want to. Or a girl may need psychological help, but she may not think she does.

How, then, do we find the need that a person recognizes—the conscious need? Is there a need that is basic to all humanity? The need for love and caring? Possibly. Yet not everyone can accept love the same way. Some have been so psychologically damaged through a sinful environment that love only pushes the hurt in deeper.

At the most basic level, however, there is a need—perhaps unconscious—for which people are willing to receive help, if the help is given rightly. That is the need to be needed.

Perhaps this brings us back to point two. In every human being is the need to be wanted, valued, and respected. In a sense this need is a God-given right, for we were created in His image.

Can a Christian need a nonbeliever? Can a Seventh-day Adventist Christian need a Lutheran Christian? A Catholic Christian? A hippie?

I tried it one day on the Berkeley campus. Walking from person to person with an informal survey (without notebook and pen), I asked a simple question to begin: "Could you help me?"

The response was overwhelming. Smiles replaced skeptical, bored looks. People opened up and talked as if I were the only one available to listen.

Approaching one fellow sitting cross-legged on the grass (engaged in transcendental meditation, I surmised), I asked hesitantly, "Could I bother you for a moment?"

Sudden radiance lighted his face. "Hey," he said softly, "I need some of that!"

People need to be "bothered" and needed. Our great God, who owns everything and needs nothing, who made everything and depends on no one, left it all because He knew that we would trust Him only if He needed us. As a babe He came into our arms helpless. As a child He was trained by one of us. Particularly for the last three and a half years, He had to depend on us for food and clothes and a place to sleep. As a human being He needed love and understanding.[9]

Can we, in this light, afford not to need others? Can we be less humble than He?

4. *He tried to break down people's prejudices.* Perhaps this is the fulfillment of all of the above, since all of them lead to breaking down prejudice. Yet we need to consider other ways to do this.

First, we should find out what a person's prejudices might be toward our view of God. Is he a devout Sunday keeper who is certain that Adventists are legalists? Is she cloudy on who we really are and liable to confuse us with some other church group? Are they afraid we may push something on them?

In order to disarm prejudice successfully, we must be sensitive to the backgrounds of many different kinds of people. We must try to understand *why* they feel the way they do. We must particularly be considerate of the beliefs they hold that they feel most defensive about.

5. *As soon as possible, He led them to see His Father in a new and favorable light.* Ellen White puts it this way: "Bring the people right to Jesus Christ, in whom their hopes of eternal life are centered."[10]

To bring people to Jesus doesn't mean merely to tell them that they must come to Him or even to tell them how to come to Him. It means most of all to tell them what He is really like and how He came to reveal the truth about His Father.

Jesus spent His entire ministry making known this truth. With our background of understanding—the history of God's love revealed in the Bible and through Ellen White—we have within our grasp a picture of God so beautiful and harmonious that we should be foremost in sharing Him with the world.

Sitting alone on the steps to the campus center one Sabbath afternoon was the very picture of Berkeley—empty loneliness, uncertainty, and apathy embodied in a lean figure with long hair falling on his shoulders.

"Hi! Could you help me?"

He looked up. A smile leaped across his face,

74

a smile that seemed to come from years past, a smile of innocence and freedom.

"I can try," he answered.

"I'm trying to find out what people around here like to read." I sat down on the steps beside him.

"Well," he hesitated, "I can't tell you what most people around here like to read because I really don't know."

"Then tell me what *you* like to read."

It was like pulling a plug. He named book after book, all of which I'd never heard of before. I gathered, though, that he was heavy into science fiction.

"But I don't know." His shoulders sagged. "I used to read a lot of that stuff, but I don't care for it so much anymore."

"Do you go to the university here?"

"Yeah. It's a big drag too."

"I understand," I said. "I wish there could be more academic freedom in colleges."

"Yeah, really!"

"Is there anything else you'd like to mention that you read?"

"Not really," he answered slowly. "Right now I'm looking for the 'Ultimate Book'!"

"The 'Ultimate Book'? What kind of book is that? A book of answers or a book of a little of everything or what?"

He shrugged his shoulders. "I don't know."

"Do you think there is such a thing as answers?" I asked as casually as I could.

Shifting his eyes to the distance, he hesitated

before answering. "Well, I think there are answers. I mean, some people are into reading the Bible, and they think they've found answers. So I guess there are some answers for some people.

"But I don't know"—defection entered his voice—"God just hasn't hit me yet."

The mental image of God with a club, hitting someone over the head—was that his concept?

"I guess I should tell you," I said, trying to keep my voice calm; "I'm a Christian."

"Hey, you should join that fellow down there," he laughed, jabbing a finger toward a young adult male dancing and singing a weird song.

"By the way, what religion does he belong to?" I asked, curious.

"Oh, some religion—I don't know—some god."

"You know," I said quietly, "what you said about God not having hit you yet interests me. Unfortunately, I think a lot of people have the misconception that Christ is going to force them to follow Him. But He never does. Instead He simply stands and calmly calls and waits for people to follow Him."

During this tiny speech, a puppy came up to my listener with a stick in his mouth, wanting to play. "Go away!" the fellow growled, kicking the dog. "Go away!"

I wondered if he didn't want interruption, or if the dog was really a symbol of me and my God.

We both paused then and waited, thinking. Then he turned to me, smiling. "Well, let me know when you find the 'Ultimate Book.' "

Standing up, I grinned back at him. "Since you know I'm a Christian, I think you know what I think that 'Ultimate Book' is."

Perhaps I should have said more. Perhaps I should have tried to persuade him to accept Christ right on the spot, to become a Christian right then and there. Or was there more to it than that?

What meaning would his acceptance of Christ have had for him if he knew so little about Him? Should we ask people to trust a god whom they think is a forceful tyrant? Should we ask people if they have the assurance of salvation before they understand what "salvation" means?

Or should we begin by trying to help them know God? Doing this takes time and effort, and I had very little time. Had I said more about God then, it might have been too much for him with his limited background.

So I pray that the seed I sowed that day will sometime later bear fruit. Adapting Paul's words, "I planted, someone else may water, but God gives the growth."[11]

Sometimes we can't finish the contact we have started. Sometimes we can't see that contact baptized. Sometimes we can only start here—with Jesus.

Notes and References

1. John 10:10, R.S.V.
2. Ellen G. White, *Evangelism*, p. 228.
3. 1 Peter 3:15.
4. Ellen G. White, *Evangelism*, pp. 228, 229.

5. John 5:6, T.E.V.
6. Ellen G. White, *The Desire of Ages,* pp. 567, 568.
7. Ellen G. White, *Testimonies to Ministers,* p. 225.
8. See Jude 8-10.
9. Ellen G. White, *The Desire of Ages,* pp. 524, 688-690.
10. Ellen G. White, *Evangelism,* p. 178.
11. See 1 Corinthians 3:6, R.S.V.

Quick Review

Directions: Mark the following that are correct.
When confronted with Satan's lies about Himself, God did which of the following:

1. Gave everyone in the universe all the evidence they needed regarding His character.
2. Proclaimed throughout the universe that He was right and Satan was wrong.
3. Submitted His case to the scrutiny and judgment of His loyal created beings.
4. Gave everyone the freedom to choose for or against Him.
5. Told everyone they'd better agree with His side or they'd eternally "get it."
6. Pleaded with Satan to realize where his course would lead and to understand that God wasn't the kind of Person he claimed.
7. Made up a long list of reasons why Satan was wrong and embarrassed him with it in the presence of his friends.
8. Gave him a list of proofs so long and so fast that it left him speechless.
9. Got everyone together to watch Him and Satan debate and argue it out.
10. Was always polite to Satan, even though He had to expel him from heaven.

When Confronted—Run, Argue, Give Up, Or—?

Dear Paul, I surely wish you could have been with me today. I could have used your help in explaining the book of Romans, particularly chapter six, verse fourteen! Why do people try to make what you wrote so difficult? Or is it that I haven't studied well enough to give a good explanation?

Had Paul been alive in December of 1975, I could have easily penned such a message to him.

It was my first day in Berkeley. I had been doing my best to keep up with Susan, my friend, as we tramped up Shadduck Avenue, then to the university campus, and down Telegraph Avenue. Now we were heading slowly back to Shadduck. I was trying to sort out all the confusing mental images I'd collected during the day, when an arm suddenly reached out with a small tract. Immediately, we stopped before two fellows, Dick and Dan, who were standing together under the eaves of a store front.

"Hi!" Susan flashed her smile. "What organization do you represent?"

"We're 'Jesus people.' "

"Oh, that's really neat." Susan tried to be agreeable. "We're 'Jesus people' too!"

Dick's eyebrows shot down. "What denomination do you belong to?"

"We're Seventh-day Adventists."

Suddenly a tornado of questions and accusations nearly swept us off our feet.

"Why do you keep the seventh day holy? That's legalistic! Don't you know that the law was nailed to the cross? We are not under law but under grace!"

We discovered that they lived next to an Adventist lady who had evidently been trying, over her backyard fence, to persuade them to keep the Sabbath.

Being immature and painfully ignorant, I tried to keep my composure, tried not to interrupt Dick, and sent as many S.O.S.'s to heaven as I could.

"Would you agree with me," I asked Dick, "that love is the fulfilling of the law? That if we truly love God and our fellowmen, we will automatically keeping the law?"

"Yes!"

"Then you would agree"—I turned to Exodus 20—"that if we truly love, we will honor our parents?"

"Of course."

"We will not kill anybody, commit adultery, or steal?" I pointed a forefinger at each com-

81

mandment. "And we will not bear false witness or covet?"

"Yes."

"You will agree further that if we really love God, we will not have any other gods before Him nor worship any graven image? We will not take His name in vain?"

"Certainly."

"And if we love God we will 'Remember the sabbath day, to keep it—' "

"Oh, no, no, no, no!"

"But you just agreed with me that if we love God we will keep the law. Why not the Sabbath?"

The funnel still swirled in an impossible twist of strange reasoning, semantics, and closed thinking.

Wow! I thought. It would be impossible to convince them of our viewpoint short of changing their thinking processes. Their reasoning seemed so illogical.

Just then Dick frowned down at me and said, "You know, you're being entirely illogical!"

Finally, all four of us were deadlocked over a few texts in Romans. Silently we stood, neither position having gained any ground. Dick and Dan stood as if waiting for something. They had run through their arguments and were out of texts. And I realized that they were ready to listen.

I hesitated to use all the proof texts I'd been taught since I was junior age, because I was afraid they would feel that the Sabbath was even more legalistic. Besides, their next-door neighbor had probably used those texts herself to no avail. Furthermore, as long as Dick's and Dan's minds were twisting the truth and were closed to it, the Bible would be of little help. Perhaps now would be a good time to try an entirely new approach.

Closing my Bible, I put both my hands behind my back in a nondefensive attitude. "May I tell you," I asked, "why *I* keep the seventh-day Sabbath?"

They welcomed my request.

"Would you agree with me that the law is a transcript of God's character? That because God's character is love and His law is love, that His law is a reflection of what He is like?"

Yes, they would agree with that.

Encouraged, I continued. "As a high school student, I worked for the registrar of the school I attended. One of my main jobs was to send copies of transcripts to other schools. Before the transcript could be sent, I had to stamp it with the school's official seal. If I didn't stamp it, the school receiving the transcript had every right to send it back. Without a seal no transcript nor any legal document has validity.

"Would you agree, then, that the law must also have a seal if it is a valid transcript of God's character?"

They nodded.

"God's seal must have His position, name, and area of rulership in it. The only commandment that has all of these is the fourth commandment; it speaks of 'the Lord' and says that He is the Maker of the heavens and the earth. If we say that the Sabbath commandment is no longer needed, how can we be sure that the law is a valid transcript of God's character? Without the seal—the fourth commandment—how can we believe that God is as loving as the law says He is?"

Looking back, I wish I would have added that the Sabbath points to God as not only our Creator, but also our Re-creator. That its meaning is bound up in righteousness by faith, freedom, and grace. That our keeping the seventh-day Sabbath is our acknowledgment that we have accepted Jesus' revelation of God and are getting to know Him better. But I needed to study more before I could really put God in a good light.

As it was, by the time I finished, Dan's head was moving in all directions; he was not sure whether to say Yes or No.

Dick simply stood silently. Then he said, "Well, I still know that you don't have to keep that legalistic Sabbath."

Just then a horn honked. Susan and I looked up in time to see the Berkeley Campus Ministries bus rolling down the next street. Motioning the driver to stop for us, we turned quickly to say a last few words.

"Why don't we keep studying the Bible for ourselves?" suggested my smiling companion.

"Yes," I agreed, "and when we study it, study the Old Testament too, asking the question:

'What does this tell us about God?' "

Dick's stunned look followed me as we hurried to catch our bus.

What more could I have done? How could I have presented the Sabbath better? These questions have puzzled me many times since. Certainly I needed more Bible study and preparation.

But I have also considered other suggestions that are basic to any discussion one gets trapped in. None of these suggestions is guaranteed to work (not everyone will accept the good news), but hopefully they will help keep tensions down to a minimum if followed.

First, *before* you get caught up in a swirl of texts and semantics, suggest to the person dedicated to setting you straight that you pray together. You could tell him that you don't necessarily have all the answers, but that God does and He has graciously given them in the Bible. Therefore you feel the need of asking God's Spirit to guide. Your being vulnerable like this may help him to be less defensive.

Give the other person the opportunity to pray first if he would like to. But don't force him to if he doesn't want to.

When you pray, pray that you will both be open to the Spirit's direction and the influence of the Bible. Pray that the discussion will be profitable and that God will stand out in His true light. (Caution: Avoid making a sermon out of your prayer; keep it brief.)

Second, if your friend is obviously very uptight about your "false" teachings, don't jump into his fire right away. Remember that "a gentle answer turns away wrath but a harsh word stirs up anger."[1] Give him full opportunity to speak his views without feeling pressured or interrupted. Smile at him and agree with him whenever you honestly can. Ask him questions, drawing out of him all of his views on his side of the problem. At the same time be as polite and respectful as possible.

Of course it takes time to do this, but it may save an eternity for the other person.

Third, when your friend has said all he can about the subject he is discrediting, ask him if you may share with him why *you* believe the way you do. Then, as undefensively as you can, give your reasons in a way that will make God look His best. Try to keep your reasons to the first person "I," and give your feelings about the subject as well as appropriate Bible passages.

For example, Mary Smith confronts you with, "You must be a terrible legalist, keeping that old Jewish Sabbath."

"Actually," you would say, smiling, "I feel perfectly free keeping the seventh-day Sabbath. In fact it's my supreme delight because of how it reminds me of the gracious way God has treated us sinners."

That's disarming and tends to turn off the burner under the boiling water.

The next step, then, if Mary is willing to listen, is to show her how all through the Bible the Sabbath is bound up with the good news about

God. (Note: Hopefully you have prepared your reasons ahead of time!)

Fourth, if you get interrupted while presenting your reasons (and you probably will), don't get irritated or impatient. Let the other person say all he wants to in objection. When he is ready to listen to you again, answer his objections as well as you can. If the disagreeing gets out of control, stop trying to answer his objections and ask if you may finish your reasons for keeping the Sabbath. When permission is granted, proceed.

Follow this procedure as many times as is necessary. It may seem tiring to you, but no one ever "wins" by shouting, interrupting, or showing irritation in any way. Your quiet demeanor alone is an argument for the truth.

One of my teachers told me once, concerning a teacher before whom I had found it necessary to defend myself, "The very fact that he tried so hard to get you to accept his viewpoint shows that he was wrong."

Even we who are so sure of certain doctrines need to be careful that our primary concern is not to *win* the argument. We may leave our "opponent" gaping, gasping, and gulping. Yet if we have put God in a bad light (and we can do this merely by putting the other party in a bad light), we have lost everything we ever hoped to gain. God will often try to cover for us, but the damage may still be eternal.

Fifth, never stoop to attacking the other party or his denomination personally. Donna (the academy student referred to in the fourth chapter) mentioned that one of the biggest deterrents to her becoming an Adventist was hearing Adventists put down Catholics.

Words like "You're simply twisting that text to meet your own opinion" may be true, but uncalled-for. That's gutter-level persuasion and is totally lacking in the courtesy with which God treats us. One can still explain the need for being unbiased without putting another down.

Sixth, don't leave the other person feeling like he's been swabbed inside and out with vinegar! Treat him with dignity and preference. Let him leave feeling as if he's still your friend. If he's still very warm about the topic, be willing to apologize for any way in which you were unkind to him. You will rarely lose his respect for doing so.

Seventh, in all the pressures involved in such discussion, never feel that you need to apologize for the truth. One of my friends, a recently baptized Adventist, was temporarily brainwashed out of the Adventist Church to join a church some of her relatives belonged to. Over the phone she gave me the reasons why she was no longer sure that Adventists were right. Sensing that our discussion wasn't getting very far, I said, "You know, truth will be here a long time, whether you and I believe it or not." That thought began to pull her out of the fog she was in.

Truth will still be truth whether or not we can ably defend it. The evidence for it is more than adequate in the Bible, and we do not need to stumble around for answers to people's objections to truth. What we need is to have those answers, not just in a list of proof texts, but in a way that makes God look good.

Our answers to all the questions people have about our message involve a God who is supremely gracious, merciful, loving, and consistent. And if we admire Him for being this way, we will seek to be like Him in all our dealings with people's doubts and fears. Our answers will clearly testify to God's thoughtful ways both by the way we speak and by our choice of words. We will be eager to testify clearly in His behalf.

There is nothing that we need to be ashamed of in the message that Seventh-day Adventists have the unique privilege of sharing with others. Never do we need to hesitate to declare that God is the kind of Person Jesus presented. We can say with Paul, "I am not ashamed of the good news."[2]

We can be proud of our God!

Notes and References

1. Proverbs 15:1, N.I.V.
2. Romans 1:16, Williams.

In the Thick of Things

Elder Arnold craned his neck to look for the address his secretary had given him. "Let me know," he told Erin and me, "if you see 20th Lane." We scanned the area as the car pushed uphill. "There's 20th Street," he announced. "That means we've missed it somehow."

Turning up a block farther and coming back down, we discovered 20th Lane. It was an alley, a dirt strip stretching between two-story apartment buildings.

After a short prayer, we headed up the alley. "Kay is in one of these apartments, I think." Elder Arnold pointed to his left. After knocking on two different doors, we finally discovered Kay's apartment. It actually faced 20th Street, but was back in behind a house. Up the creaking steps, we followed Elder Arnold to the door.

He knocked firmly.

Silence.

He knocked again.

Silence.

"I hope this is the right apartment." He

frowned. "Then again, she may not even answer."

He knocked once more.

"Who is it?" The voice coming from within was quiet but tense.

"Jere," Elder Arnold called out.

"Come in." The voice was reluctant now.

Behind the pastor, Erin and I walked into a room that was nearly dark and empty. Kay, we learned, had just moved there, and her furniture hadn't come yet.

Sitting down, we tried to begin conversation. But Kay was reluctant to talk at first. Huddled, with head bowed, she sat on her sleeping mat emotionally withdrawn. Near her lay a small bottle of pills. Beside that was the rope with which she had thought of hanging herself earlier that week.

Coming from a traumatic background, Kay had found life so depressing that she didn't feel it was worth the trouble to keep going. At different times she had threatened or tried to commit suicide. Two of those times she had nearly succeeded.

Although we tried to offer our friendship and understanding that afternoon, we weren't sure it was accepted. After we left, Kay made another attempt to take her life.

Would Kay end her life before God could reach her? Would she never be able to reach out for the evidence that would enable her to trust God? We pondered these questions during the next few months.

God didn't give up on Kay. He opened His arms wide to her, and it wasn't long before Kay became a changed, baptized Adventist Christian.

People often come to Christ when it's least expected. The moment of greatest resistance may be the moment nearest surrender. Often hostility and opposition are indications that they are fighting the Spirit's influence and, depending on their choice, may soon be at peace with God.

During such moments of stress it is best to pray, show as much love and concern as possible, and wait.

Wait. That's the opposite of pressurized soul preserving! Christ never hounds a person into eternal life. He knows that a person who would obey to keep from being hounded would have to be hounded throughout eternity in order for him to keep obeying.

"Come unto me," Christ said;[1] He did not say, "Get over here to Me, or else!" "Christ does not drive but draws men unto Him. The only compulsion which He employs is the constraint of love."[2]

God is represented as the husband who woos the homely girl to be His bride, the Father who searches for His lost son, the Friend who weeps over His enemies, the older Brother who answers Satan's charges against His siblings. Always He does the most loving thing (even when it means painful truth in kindly tactfulness). Always He does His best to *win* His rebels back.

And always He is willing to wait in patience.

How much we need patience when working to win others to Christ! Patience when someone blows up over giving up smoking. Patience when we have to repeat something we've explained at least twice before as if we've never even dealt with it. Patience when a person we've studied with hesitates ten to twenty years to be baptized.

Along with patience, we need adaptability to different situations. One person may find it hard to accept the Sabbath. Another may find giving up pork the most unpalatable part of the spiritual (and physical) menu. Some may need definite "proof texts." Others may want a more logical approach that appeals to their common sense.

Often the witness may have to switch approaches in the middle of a series of Bible studies. If a student becomes sensitive to one area, it is wise to switch to another and come back to that area later.

Or the student may lose interest. There are many possible reasons for this. Perhaps there is something deep-seated blocking his willingness to learn more about God. If there is, he may be using boredom as an excuse to avoid hearing and deciding about the topic under consideration. In such a case one may need to confront him tactfully with the seriousness of the topic involved.

Perhaps, if the student doesn't like to read, he needs some audiovisual helps such as film strips to keep his interest alive. Certainly our God deserves the simplest yet most interesting approaches available. Simple words and sentences will also increase the listener's interest.

Another reason for boredom may be that the witness has buried Christ in a tomb of arguments, texts, and data. When dealing with biblical problems such as law and grace or predestination, this often happens.

A friend of mine took a college Bible class from a teacher she really liked because of his Christ-centered approach. For two quarters she felt refreshed in his class. Then suddenly the third quarter he began leaving Christ out. Immediately she became bored and dreaded the period the class met. Soon she dropped the class, having lost interest completely.

All of our doctrines fit into the truth about God. When we leave Him out, we are not really giving our message correctly. When He is missing, the center of interest is missing. And boredom will often follow.

Paul considered everything but the knowledge of Christ "as mere garbage."[3] And Ellen White agreed: "There must be a leading along, Christ must be woven into everything that is argumentative as the warp and woof of the garment. Christ, Christ, Christ is to be in it everywhere."[4]

When Christ is the focal point of our consideration, *we* will not be so glaringly prominent. When we want Christ to look good, we will be more humble and honest. When we find ourselves without an answer, we won't pretend to have one. Neither will we put down the other person in an attempt to "win" in our theology. We may even admit that we need to study more.

Sometimes the best tack—even when one has the answer—is to suggest that both parties put aside all previous prejudices and study together, letting the Bible interpret itself. Since truth is always in God's favor, we have nothing to lose by doing this.

Certainly we can always let the student feel that his suggestions and questions are important. If he is right, we shouldn't feel that it's a destruction of our dignity to admit it. Such regard for him may encourage him to listen to us. We should especially welcome any questions he asks.

One of the greatest concerns of religious leaders and teachers throughout history has been questions. Questions make complacent people uneasy. There is something frightening about them. They shatter well-carved theological idols and yank people out of tradition-shaped opinions. Those daring to ask questions—particularly the question "Why?"—have often been ostracized as "liberals," "skeptics," "apostates," and "heretics." Yet sincere questions about God, leading to Bible study, have begun many genuine religious revivals since the time of Christ.

What should we do when a student asks, "Why did God burn up all those men who came for Elijah?" Shout, "That's none of your business!" and slam the Book shut in his face? Or welcome the question as an opportunity to share more of the truth about God?

The most rewarding Bible study I've given occurred when I asked my student what she wanted to talk about. She asked me a question about God that led us into the issue of the great controversy over the character of God. I discovered that when she asked a question, she listened better than when I assigned a topic for us to study.

Sincere questions should be our friends. God appreciates reverent questions.[5] He encourages us to reason with Him.[6] More than anything He wants our intelligent obedience and willing response. No "yes-yes" robots will be in heaven.

One morning while leading the singing for a Vacation Bible School assembly, I chose the song, "I'm in His Majesty's Army." One line of the song says, "I'm in the fight against evil like David with his stone and sling." Knowing how some children might think that Christians were literally to fight evil using such equipment, I discussed it with them.

"How do we fight in God's army?" I asked.

A little girl raised her hand. "Through prayer?" she asked.

"That's a good answer," I replied. "Are there any others?"

A little boy raised his hand. "The Bible?"

"Good! That's another one!"

Another child answered, "Jesus!"

As I agreed with their different answers, I

noted their amazement. "You mean," their faces said, "there's not just *one* right answer?"

People—especially "little people"—catch on fast to being tape recorders. When a teacher asks, "Who made the world?" the answer invariably rises back like an ocean wave of voices: "Jesus!" It sounds nice. But is it best?

In one Vacation Bible School I decided to help seventy kindergarteners learn about God the Father. I asked the same question, "Who made the world?" and got the same response: "Jesus!"

"You know who else did?" I asked. "Our loving heavenly Daddy—Jesus' Father!"

Blank faces stared back at me as if to say, "Who is He?"

During the rest of the week I tried to include God the Father in the lessons. At the end of the lesson Friday morning I asked, "Who will be the happiest to see us come home to heaven?"

"Jesus!" they all shouted.

"*And* our heavenly Daddy!" I added.

Again the same blank faces stared back at me as if to say, "Who is He?" The rut was already deep for a tender six years!

Children who aren't taught to think for themselves become adults who are afraid of questions. Perhaps the biggest problem confronting us in soul winning is that a majority of people are unwilling to change their minds from what they've been taught to believe all their lives. Their thinking is not based upon careful study but upon childhood pulpit parroting. They have never been allowed to bring out their hidden

97

doubts and questions about God, and now they may not be aware that those doubts and questions exist.

One of our biggest contributions to the world can be the recovery of the freedom in individuals to think for themselves. The truth about God invariably leads to this recovery, for God is freedom personified. He never forces a person to change his mind about Him. He never uses brainwashing methods. He doesn't want people to obey out of fear or obligation, but because they *want* to, because it's good common sense to them to do so.[7]

Jesus said, "You shall know the truth, and the truth will set you free."[8] The highest freedom comes from knowing how God treats us so reasonably and graciously and with such freedom.

If we have been set free by the truth ourselves, we will be eager to set others free. Free to ask sincere questions. Free to reevaluate former positions on truth. Free to make decisions.

The last is maybe the most difficult. It is one thing for students to take a series of Bible studies. It is another for them to make life-changing decisions about those topics!

If we have allowed them freedom all along, their decisions will be both easier and harder to make. Easier, because real decisions can be made only in a freedom-giving atmosphere. Harder, because such freedom puts the responsibility of deciding squarely upon the person who is to choose. And some don't want that responsibility.

While we should never force individuals to choose, there may be a time when we will need to make it clear to them that they should decide concerning truth. Here we need the Holy Spirit to teach us when to do this. To never bring them to this point, or even to hesitate too long, may be to pass the moment of strongest conviction. To press the point too soon may be to lose them because they feel threatened and defensive. We should always try to work within the limits of each person's background and temperament.

When the student is ready to make a decision, two things should be clear to him: (1) The decision is mine; no one can make it for me. (2) The decision is really about the kind of God I am going to worship. My decision will ultimately put me on either God's side or Satan's side of the great controversy.

Perhaps the best guidelines for helping a person to decide are given by Ellen White: "Talk to souls in peril, and get them to behold Jesus upon the cross, dying to make it possible for Him to pardon. Talk to the sinner with your own heart overflowing with the tender, pitying love of Christ. Let there be deep earnestness, but not a harsh, loud note should be heard in the voice of one who is trying to win the soul. . . .

"God wants you to have the gracious spiritual endowment [of the Holy Spirit]; then you will work with a power that you were never conscious of before."[9]

To plead in love with a person, yet let him be free; to remind him always of Jesus' picture of

God, whether it be in presenting the Sabbath or health reform—this is what it means to help a person know God.

In the thick of things—in giving Bible studies, while waiting with patience or pleading with concern—life may get tense. It *will* get exciting! Make sure, though, that in the thick of things God is always there.

Notes and References

1. Matthew 11:28.
2. Ellen G. White, *Thoughts From the Mount of Blessing*, p. 127.
3. Philippians 3:8, T.E.V.
4. Ellen G. White, *Evangelism*, p. 300.
5. Genesis 18:17-33; Joshua 4:19-24.
6. Isaiah 1:18.
7. See Ellen G. White, *Christ's Object Lessons*, pp. 97, 98.
8. John 8:32, N.E.B.
9. Ellen G. White, *Evangelism*, pp. 298, 299.

Help!

Don't go away;
I need you.
I'm not very old,
I can't grow on my own,
And sometimes
I even feel all alone.

I'm so full of questions
    and doubts—
Even fears.
This church is so new
    and strange;
Yet you seem so secure.
Please come—
Take my hand in yours.

Don't Let the New Babe Die

I had settled down to writing letters one Saturday evening near the beginning of the school year, when the phone rang. It was the dean.

"Jean," she said, "there's a girl named Carol on the second floor who is a new Adventist, and this is her first year in an Adventist school. Her mother called me this evening and is worried because Carol feels like nobody really cares about her. She's so homesick and lonely that she's wanting to go home. I was wondering if you would do something about it."

"Shall I go with her to the Halloween party tonight?"

"Yes, that's what I had in mind," the dean said, "but please don't tell her that I called."

"Sure," I replied.

Soon Carol and I were on our way to the gym for the party.

Often one of the most difficult periods in the new Adventist Christian's life comes right after baptism. To one on the outside looking in, the

Adventist Church appears to be "one big, happy family." The non-Adventist feels the warmth of continuous invitations: "Why don't you come to the youth volleyball game tonight?" "We'd like to have you over for Sabbath dinner tomorrow." "There's a city-wide youth rally coming up. Would you like to go with me?"

In the joy of discovering a new picture of God, in the warmth of Christian love and fellowship, the "outsider" stretches, smiles, and is born again. Soon he is lowered gently into the baptismal tank and comes up a radiant new creation. Members shake his hand at the door. People smile warm welcomes.

But suddenly his security blanket gets torn. The new babe wriggles helplessly into the church only to find that he's "on his own." Now he's treated as if he's been there all his life. He's automatically supposed to comprehend the complex organization of his new church. He's to understand exactly what to eat, what to wear, and how to act at all times and under every circumstance, as if his great-great-grandfather were the son of a Millerite! Confused, he runs headfirst into the "now-that-he's-baptized-we-can-sit-back-and-relax" syndrome.

But the new babe is spiritually helpless. Now that he is "in," he too is endeavoring to relax and feel at home. Consequently, he often finds himself facing a multitude of questions he's afraid to ask. Details that escaped his eager eyes before now focus as if magnified ten times. (This is especially true of those brought hurriedly in without thorough instruction.)

Church jargon is still a problem. "Whatever do they mean by 'conference,' 'the robe of Christ's righteousness,' 'the G.C.'?" wonders John New Adventist. "I've never heard before of 'quarterly services.' Why do they call their ministers 'Elder' instead of 'Reverend'?"

Other problems confronting John New Adventist involve standards and items of health reform. Suddenly he is confronted with all kinds of helpful counsel—everything from jogging to Loma Linda Foods to eating two meals a day to cutting his hair to herbs. This confusing picture looks more blurry to John if he is still struggling over giving up pork! He may find the movies still somewhat attractive. He may still feel a slight pull toward the Coors cans in the supermarket. (I still find myself tempted to believe some of Satan's lies about God.)

John eagerly grasps every bit of advice he can get (and he'll get plenty of it!) only to find he's trying to digest too heavy a diet for his young years in Christ. He's not old enough to comprehend the importance of some things and the lesser importance of others. Everything looks equally important to him—eating half a lemon at 5:30 a.m., as well as refusing to smoke!

Consequently, John may decide that the Adventists' God looked beautiful on the outside; but inside He seems to be a scowling Judge handing him two miles of computer tape crammed with rules and regulations.

At the same time, John is still trying to become

comfortable with the new truths he's just learned. "Why do Adventists find it so easy to keep the Sabbath holy?" he wonders. "I still have to remember not to drive to the ball park on Sabbath afternoons!" Or, "Ugh! This new food tastes like soft plastic! Why do they get excited about Choplets?"

Added to all this are the growing pains. When a baby is born, it is always self-centered. Its needs and feelings revolve around itself partly because it is totally helpless.

John New Adventist is not much different except that, because he is a new person, he loves others. Nevertheless, the helplessness is still there. John may feel very lonely after he becomes an Adventist. He hasn't learned yet to reach out to other people for himself; he still needs someone to reach out to him. As he becomes more comfortable with his new environment, he will become better able to initiate new friendships. But for now, he needs the support of the friendships he started out with.

During this early period of John's new life, he is probably in greater danger than he was before he joined the church. He has become somewhat comfortable with the idea "I have the truth now!" He forgets (or maybe hasn't learned) that Satan will take advantage of his newfound contentment and try to turn his eyes away from Christ and the truth to people.

Suddenly the sinful flaws he formerly ignored in Adventists slap his face hard: "There's Mr. So-and-so spitting out a swear word!" "And look at Mrs. S.D.A.-all-her-life! She's even wearing earrings!" "You know, I'm sure I saw Mr. He-knows-better going to the movies last Friday night. Why is he teaching a Sabbath School class?"

Such an attitude will seriously retard John New Adventist's growth; and, if that attitude becomes a habit, it will eventually ruin him.

Hopefully, someone will turn his eyes back to Christ and invite him to pray for the "hypocrites."

This character sketch of John New Adventist will not fit every new Adventist precisely. But certainly every new babe in Christ needs our love, understanding, and fellowship, perhaps more than he did before he was welcomed in as a church member. He needs our encouragement as he faces temptations and struggles with his bad habits. He needs consistent but tactful instruction in small quantities.

If a fellow displayed tremendous love for his girl and treated her with the respect and tenderness she'd always dreamed of, he would easily persuade her to marry him. But if, as soon as the wedding was over, he took off and practically ignored her, there would be little chance for the marriage to last.

While it is true that Christians are to be married to Christ, we are the ones who often make that marriage possible. People are often won to see God as a loving Friend because we love them. In Paul's words: "Here we are, then, speaking for Christ, as though God himself were making his appeal through us. We plead on Christ's behalf: let God change you from enemies into his friends!"[1]

Jesus told the eleven evangelists, "By this everybody will know that you are my disciples, if you keep on showing love for one another."[2]

If we leave the new babe to go on his own, he may die spiritually. If he no longer feels the warmth of our love, he may feel that Christ has also forsaken him. Many people are leaving the church today, a large percentage of whom are our peers. The biggest reason they're giving is, "I don't feel like anyone cares about me anymore."

Neglect after baptism is almost worse than neglect before baptism. It's much easier for people to go to a church they've never attended before than to go back to a church they left with bitter hearts.

So as Christian witnesses our responsibility is to love our fellow members as well as non-members. They need our warm concern, genuine understanding, and a caring that overlooks their faults.

John New Adventist may slip and fall one-hundred-plus times. Don't gasp with horror when he does. Share the hurt with him, pray with him, and help him up again.

John may tell you that he's found a new way to lose weight through self-hypnosis. Now is not the time to look horrified, run to the *Testimonies*, find the appropriate warnings concerning hypnosis, and shove them down his throat. Now is the time to patiently point out some fallacies in such a method and encourage him to put guards around his mind to keep it free to think and decide. He will only get defensive if you thunder, "How terrible! Don't you know that such a method is of the devil?"

No, John doesn't know, any more than a small child knows, without being instructed, that he shouldn't run into a street.

What will help John to grow and become mature (and we all need this) is to read, study, and meditate on the Bible for himself. He can't depend on the minister, the Bible worker, and his friends to feed him continually. Growth takes place by communion with God. Impressions, people's words of wisdom, and trials need judgment and interpretation. The safest way to get to know God is to study the Book He has given us. Otherwise one is in danger of believing Satan's lies about God.

But John may not find the Bible highly interesting to read at first. Perhaps he would rather watch TV than to read and stretch his thinking cells. Or maybe the type of reading he enjoys has more entertainment in it than truth.

That's where he'll need you—and a good modern-speech translation (I prefer the *Good News Bible* for those unfamiliar with the Bible). Show him how to read each story and chapter to discover what it says about God.

At first he may find it difficult to think that deeply. Or he may forget to look for God in it and end up reading Leviticus like a law student's text and Judges like an exciting novel. Such reading is not very beneficial. But if he persists (with your encouragement and the Holy Spirit's guidance), he may be late to breakfast some morning because he got too engrossed reading about God!

Sharing his new understanding of God with others will also help John New Adventist to grow. When Jesus freed the demoniac on the shores of Galilee, he begged Jesus to let him go with Him. "No," Jesus said, "go home and tell your people how much God has done for you and how He has loved you."[3]

Even though John may not fully understand the truth about God, he can tell what he knows about Him. That's all any of us are asked to do. And as he shares Him with others, he won't be so tempted to criticize other people or to wallow in self-pity. He'll grow up to reach out as he finds new contacts for the Lord.

As he grows, John will feel less and less dependent on you. This is as it should be. Be ready to give him the freedom he needs, and don't try to protect him so completely that he never can grow.

There comes a time in every new Adventist's life when the ropes have to be cut in order for the ship of truth to move on out to sea. Sometimes we call it "the great Advent movement," as friends move to work in new places for the Lord. Sometimes other circumstances prevent the new babe from being as close to those who once nurtured him in the truth.

God will usually direct when and how this

should take place. The new babe may not like it one bit, but someday he'll be thankful. When I was a year old in my understanding of God, He moved away my Bible teacher who had helped me a great deal. During the next three years I cried "Ouch!" a hundred times. But each hurt helped me to mature.

Unfortunately, many second-, third-, fourth-, and fifth-generation Adventists have never grown beyond the baby stage in their experience with God. These, too, need our love, encouragement, and prayers.

In essence, we need each other. Together and apart we need even more to know our God better. Then together we may all grow up into that unity resulting from our admiration of the same God.

Notes and References

1. 2 Corinthians 5:20, T.E.V.
2. John 13:35, C. B. Williams.
3. See Mark 5:19.

A Dialogue You May Want to Listen In On

SHEPHERD: Sure was a rough night last night. Lost one of my sheep.

WIFE: Just one? You've got ninety-nine others.

SHEPHERD: Yes, but even one sheep is important to me.

WIFE: Didn't you try to find it?

SHEPHERD: Didn't I? I certainly did! Wandered all over the hills, through the gullies, into the canyon. Called till I was hoarse. Even fell once. Got kind of cut up.

WIFE: Let me see— You surely did! You should let a doctor see that!

SHEPHERD: Maybe so.

WIFE: But why don't you eat first? You must be awfully hungry.

SHEPHERD: Not really. Food doesn't look good right now. If only I could have brought her home!

WIFE: You didn't even find a trace of her, huh?

SHEPHERD: Oh, I *saw* her!

WIFE: You saw her! Then why didn't you bring her home?

SHEPHERD: I called, but she wouldn't come. She just stared at me as if she didn't care at all. I came closer and she ran away. I tried and tried to get her to come to me, but—

WIFE: Well, why didn't you hook your staff around her neck? Why didn't you *make* her come to you? You're strong; you could have even carried her!

SHEPHERD: All my sheep know that I will never force them to come to me. They are free to do as they choose.

WIFE: Why didn't you follow her until she got tired and gave in?

SHEPHERD: I followed her, pleading and pleading. I wouldn't force myself on her. She kept going farther and farther away. And then—she didn't see the dropoff. I warned her. I even yelled at her—something I rarely do to my sheep. But —I'll—I'll—have to go—and bury —what's left of her—at the bottom of the canyon.

WIFE: Please don't cry, dear! You've got ninety-nine other healthy, willing sheep.

SHEPHERD: But—I *loved* her!

If the Lost Refuse
to Be Found

Recently an article I wrote on the subject of hell appeared in *Signs of the Times.* In it I showed that even when God allows sinners to be utterly destroyed, He will still love them. He will not be executing them. In mercy as well as justice, He will be allowing them to suffer the natural results of their sinfulness. Certainly, they will not burn forever, as many Christians believe.

Shortly after the article appeared, I received a letter from a reader who raised some objections to our belief that the dead are unconscious in their graves.

As tactfully and carefully as I could, I answered his letter (it took over four pages), hoping that he was sincerely seeking the truth about God. Why he (or anyone else) would want to reject it completely was a mystery to me.

Within the week that I mailed my reply, I received another letter from him. Whereas his first letter had sounded calm and sincere, his second was extremely angry and sarcastic.

As I read it I wondered, What did I say that made him react so heatedly? Why is he so angry? How could he reject such good news?

In the last part of his letter, I discovered the answer. I will quote part of it here in an edited form:

"You ask, 'How could there be no more sorrow, nor crying of the saints, if some friend or relative was being eternally tortured?' To answer this I must draw your attention again to Revelation 6:9, 10, where we find martyred saints crying to God, 'How long, O Lord, . . . dost thou not judge and *avenge* our blood on them that dwell on the earth?'

"I hope that you will particularly note the spirit or animus with which these martyred saints are imbued. They are not sitting around playing harps, sauntering . . . on the wide lawns. They are thirsting for *revenge.*

"Your idea that your relatives' suffering would make you suffer in heaven only informs me that you have not yet endured very much persecution from your unregenerate friends and relatives. Jesus promised that if you truly follow Him, the world will *hate* you. This means that your closest unregenerate friends and relatives will *hate* you and (when they get a chance) will deliver you up to death.

"That you seem not to have experienced much of this hatred from your nearest friends and relatives makes me question as to whether you yourself are *really* regenerate yet. I seriously doubt it."

Evidently, the reader felt that if I had been persecuted by my friends and relatives, I would want them to burn forever and would thoroughly enjoy watching their torment.

Aside from certain questionable psychological symptoms, I felt the letter underlined a key point as to why some reject the good news.

At first I suspect the reader was somewhat drawn to the idea of a completely loving God. But as he got closer to that idea, the light began to reveal something he hadn't thought of before. If I'm going to change my picture of God, he possibly realized, something is going to have to happen to me. If God loves those who are to be eternally destroyed, so should I. But hold it! I don't want to love those I believe are persecuting me. They deserve to die, and I intend to enjoy the satisfaction of watching them burn forever and ever!

Regrettably, if the reader doesn't change his view of God and let the good news change him, he will find out too late that God won't treat anybody that way, including the reader himself.

The rub in the good news often comes between acceptance at a distance and coming close enough to let the good news change one's life. Looking at the cross from a distance, I can say, "I like this picture of God," and yet not really accept it. But if I come close to the cross and allow its love to win me completely to God, I will say, "I love this picture of God so much that I choose to become like it." That is genuine acceptance. And the good news demonstrated on the cross is so irresistible that it will naturally lead me to this decision if I let it.[1]

If, however, as I come to the cross, I don't want to be like its picture of God, I may reject it. If I reject it, I have to harden myself against it, because the cross is the most persuasive means God uses to win me back. Its love is hard to resist.

Judas had this problem. When he felt those Carpenter's hands wash his dirty feet—hands belonging to One who claimed to be his Creator—Judas almost allowed the gracious love of Jesus to bring him to repentance. His heart "thrilled through and through with the impulse then and there to confess his sin."[2] But as he realized how far he would have to stoop to do it, his heart rebelled. He was disgusted at Jesus' gracious act, and he didn't want to worship a God who would be so humble.

Judas's god wasn't like that. Judas's god was selfish and proud, not willing to serve like Jesus. If he worshiped a God like Jesus, Judas decided, he would become degraded. The price was too high to pay, and Judas sold his God instead.

If he hadn't hardened his heart and had allowed himself to be drawn to God's love, the good news would have brought Judas to repentance. The good news would have changed him. The good news would have led him on to perfection.

But Judas stifled the love of God and decided, "I want to keep my picture of a selfish, tyrannical god so that I can continue to be that kind of person myself."

As we get closer to the end, we will find more and more people rejecting the good news. Revelation speaks of only a small group of people at the end who accept the picture of God that Jesus revealed.[3] The rest will have chosen Satan's picture of God.[4]

How are we going to treat those who reject the good news? Tell them that if they don't get with it they'll be sorry? Try to force them to accept the good news? Keep fighting back until they give in unwillingly?

How has God treated those who have refused Him completely?

He wept over Satan when He told him he could never be taken back into heaven's fellowship again.[5] He cried out to an almost hopeless nation, "How can I give you up, O Ephraim! How can I hand you over, O Israel!"[6] He cried heartbrokenly over His murderers.[7]

God has never forced anyone to accept the good news. He has never used brainwashing techniques to get His rebels back. He's never been obnoxious or worn a person down until he gives in. Reason, love, and truth are the only means He ever uses. If people refuse those means completely, He will let them go. Even then He will never insult them or be rude to them. He always respects a person's decision.

When the rich young ruler came to Jesus asking Him what more he needed to do, besides keeping the commandments, to inherit eternal life, Jesus loved him deeply and longed to save him. We can imagine the compassionate pleading in Jesus' voice as He said, "You lack one thing; go, sell what you have, and give to the poor, and you will have treasure in heaven; and come, follow me."[8]

But the rich young ruler decided that the price for the good news was too high. To worship the gracious God that Jesus revealed meant to give as He gave, unselfishly, to God and others. He walked away, sorrowful, yet in finality.

Jesus didn't run after him, begging him to change his mind. He didn't confront him with an emotional, high-powered sales talk. Through tears in His eyes, He watched him walk away.

Every person who is confronted with the good news comes to a time when he must choose "in the strife of truth with falsehood, for the good or evil side." James Lowell called it "the moment to decide."[9] That moment will keep returning as long as there is still hope for the individual. Yet every wrong decision about God makes it that much more difficult to make a right decision about Him.

Of all our powers, the power of choice is our greatest. One decision can change us and our future temporarily or even eternally.

When God created Adam and Eve with the ability to decide that Satan was right and God was wrong, He risked a lot. When Jesus came to give us back our freedom to choose His side again, He paid a heavy price. Yet both creation and redemption show us how much God values our freedom to choose.

Knowing this, we can understand how He

treats those who are deciding. God gives them the abundant evidence of His trustworthiness and love. He pleads with them all He can without overpowering them. He warns them of the results if they should choose to distrust Him. And then He steps aside. In that "moment to decide" they are in complete control of their destiny. There is no pressure from either side. Satan is not allowed to force them to his side. And God only waits. For their power to choose is the sacred area where not even God, infinite in wisdom and goodness as He is, will trespass.

If we are to witness to the God who runs this universe on freedom, we must love freedom ourselves. We must allow everyone else to be free also. Free even to say No to God.

Like God, we may cry to them, "How can I let you go?" We may warn them of what their choice will mean. But we should never be angry with them or mistreat them. We should be courteous to them and love them. We should respect their decision, terrible though it be.

The haunting plea that the fellow in Berkeley flung against Holy Hubert still vibrates in my memory: "Let me go to hell in peace!"

Heartbreaking though it seems, the most loving thing we can do for people who are determined to go away from God is to let them.

Sometimes witnessing to a gracious God may mean letting someone choose to reject His love.

Notes and References

1. Ellen G. White, *Selected Messages,* bk. 1, p. 324.
2. Ellen G. White, *The Desire of Ages,* p. 645.
3. Revelation 12:17.
4. Revelation 13:4-8.
5. Ellen G. White, *The Story of Redemption,* p. 26.
6. Hosea 11:8, R.S.V.
7. Ellen G. White, *The Desire of Ages,* pp. 575-578, 620.
8. Mark 10:21, R.S.V.
9. James Russell Lowell, "Once to Every Man and Nation," in *The Church Hymnal* (Washington, D.C.: Review and Herald Publishing Association, 1941), p. 398.

When the Door Goes Bang!

The house loomed up before me, weather-beaten and sagging, waiting for my decision. It looked forbidding to my twelve-year-old spirit, but I'd heard that colporteurs went to such places with good results. Surely a Pathfinder could too.

Squaring my shoulders and remembering my little speech, I walked up the rickety steps and knocked on the door.

Silence.

I knocked again, louder. From Sabbath afternoons of passing out *Signs* magazines, I had already acquired a knocking strategy. I would knock once, count ten seconds, knock again, count ten seconds, and knock the final time. If nobody came to the door then, I would leave.

It looked as if no one was home. The haunting aura of the house plus the wind that snatched at my Pathfinder cap almost made me leave after the second knock.

But maybe an old deaf man lived there. I knocked a third time, really loud.

Suddenly the door creaked open, and a grizzled face peered out. "Whadyawant?" the face growled.

"Good afternoon! I'm a member of the Laurelwood Pathfinder Club. We're visiting our neighbors to see if they would like to donate food for the needy on Halloween. Here's a pamphlet—"

"Idowananny!" Bang!

One look at the glaring door and I hastily retreated.

Slammed doors in winning souls aren't always literal. Sometimes they slam in the form of people who reject the good news. My father, a part-time literature evangelist, visited a lady one day who wanted *The Bible Story* and other books. However, she needed to ask her husband for permission to buy them. Before Dad got back home, our phone rang. "Tell him we don't want any of those books around here!" ordered a very irate male voice. Probably his wife was somewhere else crying. A slammed door for this reason is always very sad. About all one can do when this happens is to pray for those involved.

Other doors close because of circumstances. While in the academy, my friend Mary suggested starting a vegetarian restaurant. Her enthusiasm was catching, and soon our eager dreams began to look like reality.

The academy's assistant food service director agreed to head the project. Enthusiastically, he took us restaurant hunting. There was a vacant restaurant in the town where the academy was located. Was it for rent or for sale? We hoped it was for rent. Then a salesman who was selling the academy some products offered to donate equipment to us.

"Wow!" we said. "The Lord is really opening doors!"

Then—the restaurant we had hoped to rent was taken off the market. The salesman stopped selling his products to the academy. And the assistant cafeteria supervisor moved suddenly away in the middle of the school year.

Mary and I were left looking at three locked doors and asking, "Why?"

When this happens, it's sometimes tempting to say, "I'm never going to share the good news again." On the other hand, closed and opened doors are sometimes the only means God has of showing us what He wants us to do.

Another shut door that Mary and I encountered involved a Wayout contact, Leslie, who was a Christian. We had visited her a couple of times and had persuaded her to study the Bible with us. The question was, how and when? Leslie lived clear across town from the school. I had access to my parents' car; but according to the academy's rules, I couldn't take Mary, a dorm student, with me. Several times I tried to set up appointments with Leslie when an adult could take us; but either Mary had to work then, or Leslie couldn't be there.

Finally I decided, I'll try once more. If we can't get together this time, we'll just have to write each other.

I called Leslie, and, to my surprise, she said she could study with us that coming Sunday afternoon.

A few minutes after I hung up, Leslie called back. "Jean," she said, "I'm really sorry, but I just remembered that I have to work at the theater Sunday afternoon. So I just can't make it to study with you."

"Well, Leslie," I said, "I'm wondering if maybe we should just write each other and not try to get together. It seems to be impossible!"

"Yeah, I know," she agreed sweetly. "I've been wondering if maybe the Lord is trying to tell us something!"

Ouch!

No matter why the door closes, we should remember that it's not the end of our sharing the good news. We can find another door that will open. We can pray for more wisdom and guidance.

Also, we shouldn't always feel that just because one door slams shut, we went to the wrong house!

In a discussion group someone asked the question, "What do you do when you have to choose among several alternatives? How do you know when you've decided correctly and are on the right road?"

"Well," someone else said, "I think that you should take the road that seems right and start out. If you get any opposition, you'll know you're on the wrong road."

Whenever I think of that, I look back at the

three times I've had to drop out of college during a quarter due to unavoidable illnesses. I remember the conflicts I've had whenever I've tried to write the good news. And I seriously question that statement.

Knowing how much Satan hates the truth about God, should we be surprised at opposition? As long as he has any foothold of power on earth, he will try to stop the progress of truth. He will slam as many doors and smash as many witness stands as God will let him. But since God has already won His case at the cross, truth will ultimately triumph.

How can one tell, though, whether the opposition is coming from the Lord or from Satan?

There is no guaranteed test one can use. When a door slams shut, it is best to study the Bible and the situation, praying for guidance. Certainly the Bible doesn't give detailed instructions on how to meet every difficulty that every Christian will have to face! That's because God gave us minds to think things through on the basis of evidence and biblical principles.

But if we know God as He has been revealed in the Bible, our witnessing failures won't seem so frightening and devastating. Knowing how He has responded to the varied and often delicate situations of human history, we will understand better how and where to move ahead. Even when we're confused, we'll trust God to work everything out for the best. In His own time and way He will make our duty clear.

Perhaps the most discouraging closed doors

come from saints who interfere. For example, at a certain academy, different witnessing ventures were planned to involve its youth. Faculty members were eager; students excited. But when the proposed plans were taken to the conference leaders, the response was No.

In such circumstances, we as young people are often tempted to say, "Well, if they don't care any more than that, why should we?"

God urgently needs youth with initiative and imagination coupled with a mature understanding of God. While we should never force our way, pushing adults down as we go, we should seize every opportunity to share the good news with others. Some adults may try to hinder us, but many more will gladly help if we ask them.

When the door goes bang! it may throw us off a tiny while. We may have to wait for the noise to stop ringing in our ears so we can hear God telling us what to do next. But He will show us other doors to walk through. And then too the one that slammed shut may open later at a better time. Somewhere, somehow, God will help us give the good news.

Perhaps closed doors are really God's call for more dedication, better ideas, and greater perseverance to finish spreading the good news about God in our generation.

Consummation

(A Letter to a Friend,
Which You Might Like to Read)

Dear Debbie,

Sometimes, I'm sure, you've wondered what it would be like to be like me, a fifth-generation Seventh-day Adventist instead of a two-year-old Adventist. Perhaps you have wished you had always known the truth, had grown up with parents who understood your beliefs, had always been taught to do the right and proper things.

But, Debbie, may I tell you something? It's one thing to grow up an Adventist; it's another to know God.

Had I met you ten years ago, I would have handed you all the texts for the Sabbath and all the dos and don'ts, but I wouldn't have said too much about God. Then, He wasn't my Friend as He is now.

When I was fifteen I came face-to-face with the good news about God—that He is completely love. For a whole year I lived in the excitement of falling in love with Him. Some nights my prayers consisted almost wholly of praise and thanksgiving. The Bible became a living Person full of goodness and joy.

And then the doubts came in, the doubts I had pushed away with truth. All the misconceptions about God I'd had as a child loomed up at me with their cruel, leering faces. I struggled with my former picture of God as a split personality —love and joy on one side of His character, tyranny and gloom on the other.

Please don't think that people taught me as a child that God was a grouchy, cruel tyrant. He wasn't put in those words. It came through in the tone of voice I heard from those who talked about Him and in the lack of love and cheerfulness in their faces and gestures. It was in the emphasis on how we'd better obey or else. It was in the way Bible stories were told.

And, if nothing else, those ideas came in because God was left out. Too often He was referred to but not described. His name was mentioned, but only in passing. When the truth about God is left out, Satan is only too ready to crowd in his lies about Him.

For several years I struggled to find evidence for a fully gracious God, struggled with ingrained misunderstandings about Him. But after hours of digging my way through the Bible and Ellen White's writings, I could say, "I know that God is completely love." I could point to lots of evidence to reinforce that statement.

What freedom and joy I now have, knowing

Him as He really is! This is how I now picture Him: God is the kind of Person who has ever wanted His creatures to worship and trust Him, not because they are told to, but because they know Him to be trustworthy. He has never had anything to hide about Himself. He is open and honest, yet seeks to protect His creatures' reputations. He is fair, yet generous; consistent, yet reasonable; powerful, yet gentle; orderly, yet sensitive to beauty. Gracious and polite to the most rebellious, He patiently seeks His lost children until there is no more hope. Even when He must give the wicked up to their final destruction, He will do so with a pain-filled heart.

This picture of God is the basic substance of Seventh-day Adventism. At the heart of our message is this one most important belief: Jesus came to reveal the truth about God—that He is not the kind of person Satan has claimed. "He who has seen me," Jesus said, "has seen the Father."[1]

Without this truth none of our other doctrines would exist, for all of them are bound up in the truth about God which Jesus revealed. Our mission, then, as Seventh-day Adventists, is to declare and demonstrate this truth about God.

During the past two years, Debbie, I've tried to share with you this picture of God. I have wanted you to see Him in the best possible light. Forgive me when in any way I have misrepresented Him to you. Nothing is worse than to misrepresent God carelessly or deliberately to someone else.

We will never forget the times we spent talking about Him. It meant a lot to me to be able to share my view of Him with you.

Yet often as we talked, I wondered, What will happen when she finds out that too few church members know Him as He really is? What will she do when she hears sermons and talks in which He is misrepresented or left out? How will she feel if her peers don't understand? Will she turn on her heel and walk away? Will she become discouraged and apathetic? Will she meekly submit to the falsehoods of Satan?

I pondered these things and trembled.

Then the other day you called me. You told me that you didn't agree with a certain church member's view of God. You said you believed that when God points out people's sins He does it in love. When you told me what you thought about God, I could have sung for joy. You are learning the truth that will set you free!

Yet, as I look ahead, there is pain mingled with my joy. Oh, Debbie, to know Him and share Him as He really is, is to be lonely. Lonely even among many who call themselves Adventists, who, of all people, should understand how deeply one can feel about Him. You are already beginning to sense it. You will sense it more and more as you get to know Him better and better.

Sometimes I hear people say, "Look! Jesus is coming soon, *very* soon!" I agree; but even so, I cry with anguish, "Oh, God, Your people—they aren't ready for You to come yet! They don't really know You. They don't really care about

You." How I wish this were not true!

When you are tempted to be discouraged, Debbie, remember that He *does* have His friends in the church who understand their mission, who do their best to make Him look good. Look for them. Look more and more at Him. Then try to share Him with everybody. And love and pray for those who do not see Him as He is—even older members, peers, and pastors.

If the way gets rough in the church, please don't leave it. It is still the body of Christ. It is still "the object of His supreme regard."[2] He has great plans for it and has promised to fulfill them.[3] You will never find anywhere else a more biblical and beautiful picture of God embodied in a set of beliefs.

Someday—and I pray it will be soon—God's true people will want to share the good news about God with others more than anything else. Then the good news will go to the world as never before. John described it as a light that brightened the whole earth.[4] God's people will be radiant with His love, eager to talk about Him, prepared to answer Satan's charges against His character. In defense of His reputation, they will be more concerned that God look good than that they be saved.[5]

Not only will they speak the good news, but they will reflect it. They will no longer verbally destroy one another or gossip about and criticize each other. They will no longer treat anyone as more important than another. Instead, overflowing with a gracious God, they will treat everyone with such love, sympathy, patience, dignity, and courtesy that God will be able to come again.

Right now the stage is hidden from humankind. Lights are dim in the theater of the universe. But when God's people show that they've been changed by the good news, the curtains will be rolled back, unveiling a final part of the stage. There, before the eyes of men and angels, will be those who are qualified to speak on God's behalf.

Yet the spotlight will not beam on them. It will beam on their God as He stands in them on the center of the stage.

Keep getting to know Him for yourself, Debbie. You can talk to Him about everything in your life. Keep on sharing Him with your family, your neighbors, your friends, and fellow church members. Love them all as He would, could He be in your place.

Hold Him fast. And remember, He is holding you in hands that are stronger than death and greater than life because they bear the price for your freedom in their palms.

Love,
Your sister with the same Father

Notes and References

1. John 14:9, R.S.V.
2. Ellen G. White, *Selected Messages,* bk. 2, p. 396.
3. Ellen G. White, *Testimonies to Ministers,* pp. 32-62.
4. Revelation 18:1.
5. Ellen G. White, *The Great Controversy,* p. 619.

Love

(An Interpretation of
1 Corinthians 13:4-8)

Love lets people be free and sets no time limits for others. She never wishes to be someone else or to have what is not hers, for Love is always herself. She never flatters loving action or kind deeds or boasts of her own greatness.

Love never ignores anyone, no matter how unlovely he is. She never shoves a person to the side or leaves anyone out, but warmly accepts everyone with open arms.

Love does not insist on being supreme in anyone's life. She never complains or becomes bitter or harbors grudges. She does not rejoice when things go wrong for someone (even if he deserves it), but rejoices when things go well even for those who squander their privileges.

Love shoulders all the needs and sorrows and responsibilities in her sphere of influence. She continually wears an attitude that says, "I trust you." She hopes for the best in everything; she holds out when everyone else has given up.

Love has no boundaries. She outdoes herself without a thought. Love just keeps on.

Appendix A

WHAT SEVENTH-DAY ADVENTISTS
BELIEVE ABOUT GOD

We believe in a personal God who is intimately involved with His created beings throughout the entire universe.

We believe in a God who is three equally divine Persons (the Father, the Son, and the Holy Spirit) and that these three Persons are the same in nature, purpose, and character and are equally concerned and involved with Their creatures.

We believe in a God who is all-wise and all-powerful and is thus the very capable Creator of this universe. We believe that He created this world in six days and made human beings in His own image with the freedom to think and act responsibly.

We believe in a God who so valued the freedom of His created beings that He allowed them the opportunity to choose to distrust Him and live in rebellion against His government. We believe that, although human beings chose that option, God did not allow them to receive immediately the natural consequences of their choice but has endeavored to win them back.

We believe in a God who, although falsely accused and grossly misrepresented before the universe by Satan, has opened His case to the careful inspection and judgment of the entire universe. We believe that, through the Son's life and death on the cross, God has demonstrated His righteousness and trustworthiness.

We believe in a God who gave His Son Jesus to reveal Himself to us as the kind of God He really is so that we might be won back to love and trust Him. We believe that Jesus, being fully a man, yet fully God, was well qualified to do this.

We believe in a God who has always endeavored to reveal Himself and His plans for us, and has done so through the writings of men inspired by the Holy Spirit. These writings we call the Bible.

We believe in a God who, if we let Him, woos and wins us back to be His friends and changes us so that we become new people with new attitudes and desires.

We believe in a God who never forces us to obey or commands us to force ourselves to obey, but only asks that, because of the abundant evidence, we choose to trust and love Him. We believe that as we accept His wise instructions and continue to know and admire Him more fully, we will become like Him.

We believe in a God who so changes us and so completely buries the condemnation of our evil past that we can best acknowledge His legitimate authority in our lives by being buried as Christ was in baptism. We believe our baptism signifies that we have rejected Satan's lies about God and his dominion over us and have accepted Jesus' revelation of the Father, especially as demonstrated by Christ's death, burial, and resurrection.

We believe in a God who, in Jesus, knelt before His

disciples and washed their feet, giving us the privilege of thus serving our fellow members in Christ in a miniature baptism.

We believe in a God who wants to come into close fellowship with us and savor spiritual truth with us; therefore Jesus gave us a supper commemorative of the truths He revealed by His life and death, about His Father.

We believe in a God who is love and who asks that we keep His law of love and order, the transcript of His character, because it makes so much sense.

We believe in a God who instituted the seventh-day Sabbath as a memorial of what He revealed about Himself during Creation week and that the Sabbath has throughout history commemorated what God has revealed about Himself in all the significant events of Scripture. We believe that God has never changed His character, and thus He has never changed His Sabbath and all that it represents.

We believe in a God who, for our good, requests that we acknowledge Him as the Source of all blessings and as worthy of our worship and trust by returning to Him, the Supreme Giver, one tenth of all that He has so abundantly given us.

We believe in a God who, being a wonderful Teacher, devised a sanctuary on earth—patterned after His dwelling place in heaven—to teach men the truth about Himself. We believe that God revealed in prophecy that since the year 1844 He has been in the most intimate part of His heavenly sanctuary. We believe that, through Jesus, He is representing His believers, pleading their cases before the universe, and putting Himself on trial in them that He might be revealed to the world through their characters.

We believe in a God who, wanting us to be healthy and whole, suggests that for our good we live in accordance with His natural health laws. We believe that because God wants to fill our minds with His truth and reveal Himself through us to others, He asks that we not partake of anything which would defile His earthly temples, our bodies.

We believe in a God who wants us to be for real and free, without feeling the need for unnecessary additions to our dress and appearance. We believe that He wants us to be people with the inner beauty, security, and humility so characteristic of our gracious God.

We believe in a God who has revealed Himself and His plans in a special way to this generation. We believe that the same gracious Spirit who inspired the biblical writers has been at work among His present-day people to lead them to understand better what He has said in the Bible about Himself and about His plans for them.

We believe in a God who created man a mortal being and thus allows both sinners and righteous ones to be unconscious when they die until either the first or second resurrection.

We believe in a God who will not punish the wicked with eternal fire, but who will in love, mercy, and freedom, sadly give them up after the second resurrection to the results of their evil lives. We believe that He will allow them to be completely destroyed by fire and that this destruction is the natural consequence of their rebelliousness.

We believe in a God who will not leave the righteous in their graves but will raise them up in the first resurrection to live with Him forever.

We believe in a God who will return as the same Person He has ever been and who will—in the presence of all His living, created beings—openly take to heaven those who have fully trusted Him.

We believe in a God who, after the present earth and sinners have been destroyed, will re-create this earth for our joy and will live with us here forever.

We believe in a God who has graciously given Seventh-day Adventists the solemn yet joyous privilege of sharing these truths about Himself with every person on earth.

Appendix B

SUGGESTED PROJECTS

1. Make a list of your talents. Praying for guidance, start a soul-winning project based on those talents. Perhaps it could be something you've never heard of before. Be creative, yet use good judgment. Keep a record of what happens.

2. Experiment by starting a small Bible-study group, and personally invite some non-Adventist friends and neighbors. Go through the Bible with them book by book, asking the question, "What does this book tell you about God?" Don't push anyone to accept your ideas about Him. Emphasize that the Bible explains itself and that everyone needs to be open to new views of God. If questions naturally arise about the Sabbath or other Adventist beliefs, invite them to keep studying to see what the Bible further says about the question. Remember, though, to keep your discussions centered around the character of God.

3. Go with a group of friends to a park, wearing casual clothes. Appoint a member in your group who has a guitar to play and sing. Avoid blatantly religious songs at first. (Use songs such as "Try a Little

Kindness" and "One Little Candle.") Sit in a group, but don't act like you're part of the group at first. Play the role of bystanders. As those from the park join you, start a discussion by raising a question about God, and include them in the discussion. Have pamphlets and Bible course enrollment cards to pass out at the end of your discussion.[1]

4. Find the latest issue of the *Adventist Review* that has a list of literature requests from mission fields, and ask your pastor or Sabbath School superintendent if you might start a Mission Literature Club. Put announcements in your church bulletin (or school paper) for magazines needed, for financial help, assistance in mailing, etc. Set up a time once a month when those who wish to may help get the literature sorted, packaged, and addressed. You can get the costs from your local post office.

5. Get a project going among your friends. Ask your pastor or Bible teacher to help you get others involved too. Select a rural route or section of a nearby city, and sponsor subscriptions to a missionary magazine to everyone living in that area. Once a month visit each home which is receiving the magazine. Ask the people how they are enjoying it, and visit with them in a friendly way. See how many would be interested in further Bible study.

6. Give some money you would spend on unnecessary items (such as candy or pop), and turn in two or more names of non-Adventists you know (may be relatives) to your conference office for a missionary magazine. Write or visit these people, and ask them how they enjoy the magazines. Be open to possible interest in Bible studies.

7. Call the lay activities director in your conference, and ask for some names and addresses of people near you who are receiving a missionary

magazine or have taken correspondence courses. Get a friend to go with you, and spend a couple of afternoons each month visiting these people. Be alert for opportunities to help them. See how many would like to study the Bible with you.

8. Visit a Sunday School and mingle with the people. Join a Sunday School class and ask quiet questions that will lead the members to study the Bible more carefully. Avoid asking questions that will antagonize. Make the questions God-centered.[2]

9. Start a health venture such as a vegetarian restaurant, or get involved in such a venture already started. Try to make the venture Christ-centered, not just health-centered.

10. Find a friend who is willing to do something unusual with you. Walk together down a city street and smile at everyone you see. Write down the effects of your smiling—individual responses, etc. Do you think people could see Christ in you?[3] Do you think smiling is all that is needed to spread the good news?

11. Visit a local nursing home and get acquainted with someone who is still mentally alert, but who doesn't have many relatives or whose relatives live far away. Adopt that person as a grandparent. Visit as often as you can. Make a scrapbook, a bookrack, cookies, or something nice for the patient's room to give to your "grandparent." Read to him (or her, if you've chosen a "grandma") or take him out if you can. Confide in him your hopes and dreams. Try to talk to him about Jesus and study the Bible with him.

12. Get a good but inexpensive copy of the Bible. Buy different-colored felt pens, and begin marking passages for evidences for each doctrine (blue for the law, red for second coming, etc.). Don't be afraid to write in the margins. Make this your Bible-study workbook.

13. Make an outline for a Bible study for each of our beliefs, fitting them into the framework of the good news about God.[4]

14. Make a list of people who do not know God very well. It can include anyone (some Adventists need to know God too). Pray for each person every day that God will help him discover the truth about Him. Keep open to opportunities to help these individuals. Make note of the times when God uses you to help answer your own prayer. At the end of a period of time (say, three, six, or twelve months), write in your diary any progress you see in the persons you've been praying for. If nothing seems to have changed, don't give up. Keep praying.

15. Do some research in connection with the above project, answering the question, "Since God loves everyone and longs to win everyone to Himself that He can, why does praying for a person help him?" Some helps might be Zechariah 3:1-5; Revelation 12:10; Job 1, 2, 42:7-10; John 16:26, 27; 17; James 5:16. Note Ellen White's comments on these passages.

16. Form a secret club (maybe in dorm or neighborhood), or make yourself the "club." Give it a secret name and do nice things for people without being identified. (For example, some girls living near my room in a college dorm gave 3 x 5 cards to other girls with encouraging handwritten messages and promises.)

17. Write your personal experience about how you came to know God (for example: "I used to think of God as _____ but now I see Him as _____). Practice telling it until you feel comfortable with it. See how often you can work it into everyday conversations without it sounding out of place.

18. Start a "chain" letter among your friends, de-

signed to share your experiences with Christ and to encourage one another. See how many non-Adventist acquaintances you can add in time.[5]

19. Buy a copy of a book designed for non-Adventists that puts God in a good light. Write your name and address in the back cover with the note, "If you would like to know more about God, please let me know." Put it in a place where it is likely to get picked up. If someone answers the note, respond to it. Send him a subscription to a missionary magazine or tell him about our radio and television ministries. He might like to take a Bible correspondence course.

20. Go to a public place (a park, university campus, etc.) with someone else, and ask people to help you. Questions you might ask are: "Do you know where the _____ is?" "Could you please tell me what time it is?" Note the looks, actions, and words of the people you talk to before and after you asked them for help. Report what happened to another friend.[1]

21. Get the little children together who live near you, and hold a Bible story hour. You might want to check at your conference office for aids in starting a Neighborhood Bible Club for children.

22. Offer your services in a children's Sabbath School division. Remember, S.D.A. children are souls who need winning too!

23. Get your friends together, and make one Sabbath of each month a day to visit shut-ins and bring them a short Sabbath School.

24. Form a committee of willing friends, and think up ways to acquaint the neighborhood surrounding your academy or college campus with a positive picture of the God of Seventh-day Adventists. For example, you could (with the permission of key faculty members) make up a brochure explaining what the mission of Adventism is and why it believes in Chris-

tian education. Include appropriate pictures. Give people a chance to request certain services (for example, a tear-out form they could mail in, on which are boxes to check beside such items as "I would like to know more about your view of God" and "I would like to attend a Five-Day Plan to Stop Smoking"). Mail the brochures, or pass them out. Think up other ways to acquaint your community with your God.

Notes and References

1. One word of caution for when you go to a park or university campus. Always keep a friend you know well in view if you leave your group. If anyone tries to draw you away from where you are to a bus, camper, other group, etc., be on your guard. If he tells you he is a Christian, find out exactly what church he represents. Even if he appears clean-cut, be careful. My reasons for stressing this are valid. While in Berkeley I was approached by a nice-looking young couple who told me they were Christians. They persuaded me to go with them to their makeshift "restaurant" in a van. Then they tried to get me interested in attending a retreat at their special community in the country designed to teach people how to live in peace and love and unity. I realized later that they were probably members of a cult which often brainwashes its initiates.

2. If you're in doubt about the rightness of doing this, see Ellen G. White, *Testimonies for the Church,* vol. 6, pp. 74, 75.

3. You might carry short, appropriate pamphlets with you in case you get to talking to someone who is interested in the good news.

4. See Appendix A for ideas.

5. For safety it's best to write to those who are of the same sex.